O. von Barchwitz Krauser

Six Years with William Taylor in South America

O. von Barchwitz Krauser

Six Years with William Taylor in South America

ISBN/EAN: 9783337315498

Printed in Europe, USA, Canada, Australia, Japan

Cover: Foto ©Andreas Hilbeck / pixelio.de

More available books at **www.hansebooks.com**

Six Years with William Taylor

IN

SOUTH AMERICA.

BY

REV. O. VON BARCHWITZ-KRAUSER.

Published for the Author, by
McDONALD & GILL,
Office of the Christian Witness, 36 Bromfield St.,
Boston, Mass.

INTRODUCTION.

Steamship "Ilo," Pacific Ocean, }
August, 1885.

For some time it has been my wish to tell the friends of Bishop Taylor, and those interested in the progress of his "Self-supporting Missions," what God has done for me, while I was so privileged to preach the Gospel in Chili, South America. The time seems to have come now, and although on board the steamer, yet it seems to be the proper time to say something on the subject. My heart is so full, and I must unburden myself to the honor and glory of God, as I trust it may be. Of course I was looking for a beginning; but so many thoughts of difficulties crowded into my mind, which, indeed, seemed to baffle my intention from the beginning. One fact seemed to trouble me much, and this was:

"You can't write in English,— you have never studied that language, and you know nothing of the grammar and — you might do in speaking it, but to write in English, — you had better not do it." In all this I seemed to hear a whisper, and that whisper I did not like; I thought I recognized the cloven foot, and the voice of the infernal one. So I knelt in prayer, and then the Comforter came, and a voice seemed to say: "Write; I will bless thee. Write as best you can." Then the thought came to me: "There is so much said just now about Bishop Taylor and 'Self-supporting Missions,' that it might appear to be in time, if I, too, would say something of what God has done in Chili, to help along the cause, and, above all, glorify my Father which is in heaven. This being my sole object, this little work will, in every other respect, be quite unpretending.

Now, in reading over what I have just written, I see that this might stand so, and answer as an introduction. In the name of my Redeemer I shall go on, earnestly praying that the richest of blessings may attend the reading of this little book, and that the Saviour may be glorified in the face of all who wish to know how God blesses those who will trust Him for all things, and how He blessed me and kept me, soul and body, during the six years of self-supporting labor for Him.

THE AUTHOR.

CONTENTS.

CHAPTER I.
MY CALL, AND WORK AS AN EVANGELIST IN NORTH AMERICA.

Pushed out on a self-supporting basis—A church in great distress—Holiness preaching—How the Lord sends the supplies — — — — — — — — — — — 11

CHAPTER II.
SUMMER AND HARVEST-TIME REVIVALS.

A remarkable answer to prayer—A blind man with good eyes—A wonderful experience—He careth for us—Midnight grace—An experience in selecting a text—How the Lord slew a Goliath—Filling out a number of blank checks—Martin Luther's ink-bottle—a comparison — — — — — — — — — — — 37

CHAPTER III.
MY FIRST MEETING WITH BISHOP TAYLOR IN 1879.—DAYTON CAMP-MEETING.

A visit to the place of my birth—His grace all-sufficient—Struck in the face; glory and praise—In a prison—Justification and entire sanctification inside of fifteen minutes, 65

CHAPTER IV.
MY CALL TO SOUTH AMERICA.—A LETTER AND A VISIT FROM FATHER TAYLOR.

A visit from William Taylor—Leaving for South America—The first revival in South America—Life on the Isthmus—On the great Pacific—First money earned in Chili—Bro. Smith preaches to the natives — — — — 82

CHAPTER V.

ON THE BORDERS OF NORTHERN PATAGONIA.

Landing on the field of battle — My first German sermon — The colony on Lake Llanquihue — How my landsmen live — The new idea : a holy man — First signs of opposition — Their forlorn condition — A conference - - 100

CHAPTER VI.

THE COMMENCEMENT OF WORK IN THE COLONIES.

The first convert — Taken prisoner — A missionary's pleasant trip to a wedding — The conversion of ten children — A Roman Catholic family converted to God — A trying change — A sure way to get bad roads repaired - - 118

CHAPTER VII.

A CHANGE TO THE CITY.

A wonderful deliverance on horseback — In Osorno — My first funeral sermon — Preaching to natives — Among the children — Polite with dogs - - - - - 140

CHAPTER VIII.

MY CALL TO VALPARAISO. — LEAVING THE COLONIES.

Good common sense - - - - - - - - 157

CHAPTER IX.

A RICH MINE DISCOVERED. — GOING TO WORK.

Prayer-meeting in a bar-room — Shot behind the counter — Collared by a woman — The main-top — How God saved a rum-seller — A remarkable conversion — Good for a beginning — Native work — A native converted — The priests after me - - - - - - - - - 162

CHAPTER X.

IN THE HOTBED OF VICE AND CRIME.

A dancing-house proprietor in close quarters — How to manage — Attempt to cut his throat — Hunting souls — A terrible death - - - - - - - - - 183

CHAPTER XI.

Times of Special Visitation.

An aged drunkard converted — Organization of a Good Templars' Lodge — A Sailors' Home is called into being — An ex-rum-seller becomes the administrator of the Sailor's Home — Opinions of some ship-masters — A street meeting in front of a brothel — A bit of advice — How I paid a debt — Tobacco experiences — Prayer on a jibboom — In the jaws of death — Deciding for Christ on the gangway — Be sure your sin will find you out - - - 196

CHAPTER XII.

In the Fiery Furnace with Jesus. — Unexpected Changes.

The Gospel for the natives — Shadows of the valley — A struggle for light — My German Methodist Church — A trip to the old "Vaterland" — One taken, the other left — The Methodists in Uruguay and the Argentine Republic — Rio Janerio — Thirteen years ago an infidel — Days of power in England - - - - - - 223

CHAPTER XIII.

Across the Channel, Homeward Bound. — The Revival in Germany.

Heaviest trials and brightest sunshine — My children, both gone to be with Jesus — At the grave of my sainted mother — Preaching in Berlin — The power of love — A remarkable feature — Confession of sin — A daughter brings home her wandering parents — Ashamed of Christ — The experience of a dressmaker — Snatched from the burning — Satan on development — A remarkable experience in fasting - - - - - - - 242

CHAPTER XIV.

East Prussia. — The Ancient City of the Kings.

In the right spirit — A Methodist old-fashioned meeting — Rioters made friends — The day of Pentecost had fully come — The ancient city of the Kings — Kant's city - 270

CHAPTER XV.

MY RETURN TO CHILI, TAKING WITH ME A GERMAN COLONY.

The father of a large family of big "little ones" — Crossing the Coast-Cordillera — The new Colony — Settling the Colonists in their new homes — The needs of Valparaiso — Divine services at the Colonies   284

CHAPTER XVI.

THE FUTURE OF CHILI. — SOMETHING ABOUT THE LAND AND ITS PEOPLE.

Needed workers — Bishop Taylor's mountain goats   296

CHAPTER XVII.

MY PERSONAL EXPERIENCE. — WONDERFUL SALVATION.

Early religious training — The influence of my mother's life — My infidelity shaken — trying to get away from God — A broken-hearted mother — In America — Sick and in rags — Light from Calvary's cross — A personal fight with Satan — The terribleness of sin — The discovery of a hidden enemy — The repression theory — The disappointment — A prisoner gives me the "Guide to Holiness" — A real inwrought holiness   310

Six Years with William Taylor in South America.

CHAPTER I.

MY CALL AND WORK AS AN EVANGELIST IN NORTH AMERICA.

The following extracts are from my journal, which I have kept from the day on which God called me to preach the Gospel as an evangelist, and long before I knew anything about William Taylor and his work.

I read there the following: —

Indianapolis, May 18, 1878.— On the 18th of May, 1878, after earnest prayer, I felt called to go and preach the Gospel. When the Lord saved me from the jaws of death, and converted me so wonderfully in 1874, I promised Him that I would preach the Gospel. To-day Jesus came to claim me and take me at my word. I immediately left my occupation, and on speaking to a dear brother — G. Haines — about it, he told me that the Lord had also much impressed him for days, and that he had much thought about what the Saviour did when he sent out His apostles, "two by two." "I was waiting for some more definite instructions from the

Lord," said Bro. H., "when you just stepped in, and I believe the Lord would have us start out together."

We rejoiced to be thus confirmed concerning the will of God, and, kneeling in prayer, we consecrated ourselves anew to God, waiting to be filled with the Holy Spirit for the work that was set before us. Oh, that precious hour! How can we ever forget it! There was no more fear; if there had been any as to the certainty that God had called us to go out, it was certainly gone now. It was a moment of great importance to us. We felt it deeply, and our humiliation was complete. If ever we felt our own weakness, it was now; but God, our strength, appeared, — the Lion of Judah on our side we felt, and were safe.

At 12.40 P. M., the same day, we left for Z——. In the train we talked together, and recounted the dealings of God with us in the days gone by, and we found to our great satisfaction and joy that the Lord did not send us on short notice; but that He had tried and sifted us quite thoroughly in preparation for this distinct call; and no wonder that when it came we were found ready to say, "Lord, here am I, send me."

Pushed Out on a Self-Supporting Basis

Next came up a question which neither one of us had thought of until now, and that was *our support;* to be sure it did not come to us as if it were questionable, although with some good people the devil gets a start on them thus far; but it came in the shape of a joyful thought, to be "privileged" to trust the Lord and never to ask help; and next, never to take up a collection. It took but a few moments to skip over that ground, and we were floating away in the land of perfect trust on that line.

Bro. H., with a beaming face, told me then that he had but very little of the (to some people) eye-blinding or all-engrossing shining metal. I, being in possession of only forty cents, did not say a word, for fear (not the ashamed kind), of shouting outright in the cars. The Lord gave me plainly to understand, on starting out, that He would have me go on the apostolic line of self-support, the "faith line," as regards personal support, — traveling expenses, clothing, etc. The Lord gave me a "blank check" to all His provision stores, clothing-houses and hotels. I felt that I need only fill out the check and draw on Him for all my necessities. When this was pressed into my hand, it seemed tangible, and tears ran down my cheeks; and silently I pressed the hand of my Bro. H., who sat at my side, drinking, as it appeared, at "the fountain deep and wide."

As yet, we did not know how the Lord would lead us on our way to the people of Z——. Indeed, we could not arrive at a definite plan, and had to give it up, because the train had just stopped; and, leaving the depot, as by common consent, we made for the woods, which looked so inviting to us, at a little distance before. We concluded that there was the place for us to have a little conference with the Lord — the Father, the Son, and the Holy Ghost. It was not long before we knew the triune God had come "our souls to greet," and, there in the woods, "glory crowned the mercy-seat." (It struck me then that some people don't know that, according to circumstances, the Father moves the mercy-seat into the woods.)

When we arose, Bro. H. had his instruction. Looking at me he said: "Bro. Krauser, I remember having heard the name of the preacher in charge in this place, and if this is Bro. C., with whom I traveled fifteen years ago on the same circuit, we shall have no trouble to get a place for our meetings, and get the people, too."

We went straight to the house of the preacher, having inquired of some one in the street as to its location; but it was the house of the local preacher, who told us he thought it the wrong season of the year for protracted meetings. We told him that we had received marching orders, and that we did not believe the Lord had made such a mistake as to send us in the wrong season of the year; but knowing the history of "revivals in their season," on the whole we did not mind what our good brother had to say, but begged him kindly, to conduct us to the house of Bro. C., which the man did. We soon found Bro. C.'s, the door opened, and the recognition of my partner and Bro. C. was mutual. They were, indeed, old acquaintances. The house was at once put in shape to keep us for a few days, and arrangements made for what was to be the first meeting on our evangelistic tour, and of course we were hopefully looking forward and upward to God to put His seal upon this, our first effort to save souls.

Bro. C. had made us aware of the sad fact that it was a "stronghold of infidelity," so Bro. H. announced a "temperance meeting" for to-morrow (Saturday) night. The rest of the day we spent in prayer and reading the Scriptures.

Saturday evening, May 19. — My heart is lifted up to God. My soul rejoiceth in God my Saviour for this night's work. Bro. H. got off his temperance speech. The place was crowded, and the moment seemed to have come to preach the Gospel before closing the meeting. The Lord blessed me in delivering my message, and strong conviction was produced, as could be noticed if one but for a moment looked over that congregation. At the close I gave out meetings for the following day, which was Sunday. Three meetings were to be held — at 10.30 A. M., 2. 30 P. M. (Gospel temperance meeting), and 7.30 P. M., (preaching). After the meeting many came to me, and with tears, confessed how they had backslidden, and some said that they would like to be converted to God. The spirit of the meeting seemed to have taken them unawares, — they appeared to be confounded and confessed that to-night they were not ready. Poor souls! They then expressed a wish that we would remain, and that the Lord in mercy might lead them to repentance unto life. God grant it. Amen.

Sunday, 20th (*evening*). — What a glorious day! Early in the morning we retired to the woods, and there talked with God until it was time to open the church. I had selected for my text the words in Ex. xii. 13. How the beams from Calvary's cross laid open before me the unspeakable wisdom of God, as revealed to me in the "great book"! A storm was brewing, and everybody seemed to feel that soon a "break" must take place, and we were looking forward in faith and hope. No altar work had yet been introduced; but it was soon to come.

The afternoon meeting was one of great power. Bro. H. preached a Gospel temperance sermon. Oh, how the power of darkness strove against light! I remarked to Bro. C. that I had never before felt such an opposing power prevail in the very atmosphere. It seemed he had felt it, too. But one soul found rest after a hard struggle for freedom. A drunkard came and yielded himself up, and also signed the pledge. The poor wife, who was sitting in the church, could not contain herself longer; she arose, and coming up to the altar, fell about the neck of her husband and both wept tears of joy. It was a heart-melting time, and God was using this to melt the hearts of some who had become hardened.

In the evening service, two stood up for prayers. Step by step, the ground had to be taken; indeed, the stronghold of infidelity had to be assailed.

On Monday, one sister came forward to the altar, and arose, praising the Lord for salvation found. Tuesday morning we retired again to the woods, and the Lord gave us a precious baptism of power, and as we had announced meetings to be held during this entire week, and three meetings a day, we opened to-day at 10 A. M., and preached on Christian perfection.

It was evident what was wrong in that church, and to-day it should not only be revealed, but the hurt was to be healed. While I preached to the members of the church, Bro. H. went into one corner of the church and there hid himself with God, and stayed during the entire service, and only came when the altar was crowded with seekers, to work among them. Among the seekers ofter holiness, was the pastor of that church and his wife. The dear brother had been preaching for thirty years, but arose and confessed, that such manifestations he had never beheld before; and with holy joy, and the imprint of a heavenly, perfect peace, beaming from his face, both he and his wife confessed to have obtained the blessing of a pure heart.

Ten days we stayed in that town, and the blessings that now followed may easily be imagined. Several were freed from the power of sin — of unbelief — and the tower of the infidel was undermined; and the best of all, our Bro. C. was now prepared to go on with his work, and we hope his church to-day is flourishing.

Now, all this time we had not been asked, "Who supports you?" but as they had found out who sent us, we had no doubt but that the same would give us the money we needed to continue our journey. We also had not said a word to anybody on that subject, — nor did we take up any collections. We had told Bro. C. that the next town, about five miles distant — W. —— — we had chosen for our field of operation. He begged us to desist from it, and change our plan, and gave as his reason for advising us thus, that the poor brother who had been in charge of the church there up to only a few weeks ago, and who once enjoyed the grace of God, had sadly fallen, and the whole church was on the point of dissolving membership; and that the few remaining faithful ones were completely discouraged. We were quiet — not saying a word; but before starting for the railway station we once more made for our favorite spot in the woods, where the Saviour so often had met and communed with us, and told him all about W——. The more we prayed, the more we became certain of going to that place. It had become evident to us that the poor people in W—— had been quite forsaken, and in their extreme distress had not had the comfort of Christian counsel. However, God remembered His church in W——, for He had yet a few there, who had not bowed their knees to Baal.

A Church in Great Distress.

We hurried back to Bro. C. and told him we had orders to proceed at once to W——. He bade us Godspeed, and we departed. I took my very small hand-satchel, and felt in my pocket for the forty cents;— just ten cents lacking to pay a five-mile fare. I felt I could not ask Bro. H. to help me out; and, besides, I knew he had but enough for himself; and yet I knew I was to take that train that was to come around the bend in about ten minutes.

While Bro. G. was talking with some one on the street, I hurried on to the depot, deposited my satchel with the ticket-agent, telling him that I would be back in a few minutes, and opening the back door, I looked for a place to pray once more to God; but finding an open space, I remained standing in the open door, and crossing my hands behind me, I bowed my head in prayer to Him who had told me that He would supply all my needs. I filled then and there a blank check, and presented it at His bank. I drew on it for only ten cents; it was all I needed at the time. Suddenly I felt some one taking hold of my hands behind me; and, making an effort to turn, I beheld Bro. C., the preacher of Z——, and at the same time I felt him pressing something hard into my hands. With tears in my eyes I opened the hand, and in it was a bright new fifty-cent piece of silver,— to pay my fare, the brother said— and "I felt you needed something, and so I ran down before the train came to give it to you— and— there it comes now; run and get your ticket!" I had no time to say a word—I only ran and got my ticket. Bro. H. got his just then, too. We got into the car, and with a hasty "good-by" and "God bless you," the train started off again. This whole transaction took place in just the shortest possible time, so that not until the train had started did I begin to draw breath and look over the situation. It was a most pleasant one to be in, to be sure; and, praise the Lord, I could say, with all my heart, God had again sent us. Amen! I had asked for ten cents, but the Lord sweetly humbled me by sending me fifty.

In the cars I opened my satchel to arrange some things, and found that Sister C. had put in one new shirt and some other little things, she thought I needed. The Lord knew I had but two shirts, and one of these I wore at the time. Now, I thought, it is so sweet, and such a wonderful privilege thus to trust Jesus. We sang, "The Lord is my Shepherd, I shall not want." No, not any good thing will He withhold from them that trust Him; how much more, then, shall He not withhold the things we need.

Saturday it was when we arrived in W——. We called at once on Bro. I., who was one of the officials. Found him much discouraged, indeed, and, like a drowning man, he took hold of this opportunity of reviving the church. Indeed, he was a faithful officer. We again retired to the solitude of a pine-tree forest, close at hand, and made our plans before the Lord, and His blessing attended us.

That same evening we opened the church to the people, and at the close of the meeting we announced three meetings for the morrow — Sabbath. A few trembling brothers and sisters had dared to come out. Also a few from the Lutheran church, who, however, manifested a considerable amount of earnest enmity and jealousy; for they, being afraid that the church might build up, threatened to burn the building if we continued preaching. We did not fear, but met again for service at 10.30 A. M. on Sunday.

Bro. Haines preached to a filled house. Thank

God, the people came out to hear, although sneered at by many standing outside, and crowding the door, who dared not come in. The season was one of great power. After preaching, Bro. H. asked me to exhort the people to come to the altar and seek the Lord; and the disheartened, or backslidden, to come and meet with us in earnest prayer. The Lord blessed this invitation, and *seventeen persons came forward!* all seeking the Saviour. Bro. H. had preached from Rev. xxii. 14, and it seemed the tree of life was spreading its branches to receive the church back under its protecting shadow. What a meeting! It is true, bitter tears of repentance flowed then, but it was a repentance not to be repented of, and two precious souls found the Lord, and soon were praising Him aloud for His goodness and mercy. Another struggled hard, and truly in pity the Lord must have looked down upon that poor woman, for she was a great sinner, and she would not let go the Lord until He had blessed her. Surely such determination will meet with a determined Saviour.

In the afternoon I preached from Isaiah ix.: "The Wonderful." Three persons again came forward, and gave themselves to Jesus.

The town was stirred thoroughly by this time. The Lord evidently meant business, and would build up that church in spite of Satan and his agents.

Bro. Haines preached in the evening on "Eternal

Life," and I followed with a few words from Exodus: "Stand still and see the salvation of the Lord." Two persons came to the altar for prayers, and while they were praying for deliverance, a sister stood up in the congregation and declared that now, this moment, Jesus saved her from her sins.

HOLINESS PREACHING.

This meeting was one of the most powerful that we have had in this church. Tongues failed to express it during the meeting. Holiness as a definite blessing subsequent to conversion was now preached, and this seemed to be striking the keynote and lifting the dear people up and out of the misery of a half-consecrated life. The reason why the Lord had permitted them to be so sadly tried during the past, and why it seemed as though all hope was cut off, was made clear to all. The testimony of a blood-washed throng of seven precious souls rang up to heaven in one great hallelujah to God. The very foundation of the church in which we were pleading with God for never-dying souls, seemed to quiver and tremble because of power flooding the hearts of those precious brethren. Most had left, on that day, their work out in the field, wanting only to settle the question with the "Mighty to save." Oh, that day! a day never to be forgotten in the annals of that church. Here are some of their testimonies: —

Sister L.: The blessed Jesus saves me now, this moment. Yes, He doth give me a clean heart; I know it now. Amen.

Sister R., an aged sister: I have served God according to the best of my knowledge; but oh, I never saw in all these years such wonderful light as at present. I always knew and felt there was something better for me than what I had; but I never found just how to attain to such an experience as I possess now. Thanks be to God, to-day I see it plain, and now Jesus has released me from sin, and all fear is gone, and I know He saves me fully. Oh, what sweet peace has come to my soul! Now it is all glory, glory, glory! (This sister, while pleading at the altar with her Saviour, seemed to have left the body for a time; then suddenly her face began to shine, as it were above the brightness of the sun. Just then I looked at her face, and I seemed unable to take my eyes off. I never saw such a glory upon a child of God before. She then clapped her hands and said softly, "Oh, Jesus, Jesus, blessed Jesus!" Oh, how my soul magnified the Lord to be permitted to see the works of the Lord, who saved also me; whose precious blood had also reached my own heart, and proved sufficient even in my case. I wept and laughed in turns because of joy.)

Next a Lutheran sister — Sister E. — got up and said: I have served God, or have been trying to serve Him, for many years; but ever since my conversion I have been troubled with an unsacrificing spirit. It seemed a cross to testify for Christ. Soon I discovered other besetting sins. But now God has delivered me, and also cut loose my tongue. Now I shall praise God as long as I live, for this is new life I have received. Now, pray for my children, that they also may be saved.

Bro. K.: I have known God many years. God converted me and pardoned the sins of my past life; and I have enjoyed many seasons of rich blessing. To-day, dear brethren, I have got something I have never had before — a clean heart. Jesus sets me entirely free. Oh, praise God for a complete deliverance from all sin! I am now entirely His property.

Bro. S.: God has kept me through all the storms of the last war, and then it was that I promised the Lord that I would serve Him if I should be spared long enough. Long afterwards, not far from the spot where I now stand, I gave my heart to Jesus. I served Him the best I knew how; but when walking behind the plow in the field, if the horses would not go just right, I would often "fly off." Many times I was on the mountain-top, and next down again in the valley. I felt it to be a constant struggle, that seemed to be not of the right kind; and then, when walking behind that plow, it would strike some hidden root, which caused the horses to be jerked back; and while trying to clear the plow the poor animals would step over the traces. Before getting them back I would "fly off" and get angry with the old stump, whip the horses, and then hide behind some tree in shame, and in tears ask God to forgive me. There was something wrong. I see it to-day. I never had heard of this doctrine before,— this perfect love — heart purity; although I longed for something like it; but to-day this talk just fitted me. I saw the light, and a clean heart I must have; and thanks be to God, Jesus cleanses me now from all sin,— takes away everything contrary to Himself. I can now fully trust Him to keep me from falling. (This brother wrote afterwards to the *Harvester* that the Lord had also saved him from the filthy use of tobacco.)

Bro. U.: I remember with much pain how I used to hide from my class-leader or preacher, although attending all the meetings, simply for the reason that I feared to stand up and testify. Now, can we call that *enjoying* religion? I tell you it was a misery to me to live thus; but to-day I thank God, He has given me a clean heart; He takes away from me now this slavish, man-fearing spirit. I trust Him fully. Thank God!

Tuesday. — The fire is still burning. Sister H. went out to buy some groceries, but could not pass the church, but "just came in for a little while." The Lord brought her to seek Him, receive Him, and confess Him. The groceries got home somewhat late, but the precious soul got saved just in time. Another Lutheran sister gave her heart to Jesus.

The meeting was closed, and when we reached our lodging, we heard a great noise in doors. Opening the door, I saw a good woman laughing and weeping for joy, because she had just found Jesus, at home, while we were at church.

In the evening we gave place to a temperance society which had existed some time in the place. However, I was invited to attend. The president was a professed unbeliever, and there were many attending that meeting who were not in the habit of attending religious meetings. That evening the Lord had something in store for them all. The sister whom the Lord had converted at her house, this afternoon, came to the temperance meeting; and finding certain of her friends there, she was unable to be quiet. She went up to them, when they were seated, and, shouting and praising God with a loud voice, she told before the multitude what God had done for her. She was a young lady of seventeen. The temperance meeting was formally closed, and it was turned into a Holy Ghost meeting. Others began to praise the Lord with a loud voice, and at last I could not keep from shouting outright. It seemed that the Spirit of God had gotten hold of us, and if we had refrained from praising God, the very stones would immediately have cried out. All prayed and praised the wonderful Jesus, and all prayed, "God save the people." Thus closed the temperance meeting.

Wednesday morning, at 10 A. M., we met again at the church, and the Lord graciously poured out His Spirit upon those assembled, and six persons came forward for prayer. Among those at the altar were two little girls of twelve years. In speaking to them, while kneeling, I was struck at hearing them clearly defining their condition. They knew what they wanted. I felt sure the Lord would answer their prayer. Soon the power of God was manifested. One of them arose, praising Jesus for salvation just found, and walked about shaking hands with all present, and shouting aloud. The first time I ever heard a person of her age shout. It did me much good. We saw her then leave the church in haste, and while the others were yet speaking, giving their testimonies, our little sister returned, leading some one by the hand, and said: "This is my older sister. I ran home and told her what the Lord had done for me, and that I wanted her to come and seek the Lord at once." Having thus spoken, they both knelt down to pray. The congregation, much affected by what they had witnessed, also knelt, and soon the other sister was made to rejoice in Christ her Saviour. A few days before both the parents of those girls were converted to God. We see here a clear fulfilment of the word, "The promise is to you and your children." Dear parents, lead the way, and your children will follow, if your conversion is genuine.

One brother professed conversion, while his wife, kneeling beside him, praised God for a clean heart. But this poor brother, before we left W., had gone back to the world — and why? He had lost a cow, and began to grumble, and lost his temper. His wife told me his farm and cattle had always been the man's besetting sin. Shall riches satisfy the soul? Oh that man might see what it profiteth to "gain the whole world and lose his own soul"! An old cow had tripped him. The day will come when some who saw the wonderful work of God in this place, and wilfully neglected to improve the time of this special visitation of divine grace, would give gladly all they possess in this world to get a berth, however small, in the old Noah's ark, which they now would not buy even for kindling wood if offered at auction. Some people talk about Judas. Why, some sell their master for a drink, or for the mere sake of appearances, or for oxen and sheep and fashion.

One of the young ladies at the altar found it hard to give up fashion. Oh, how bewitching a thing it must be, if, in trying to take hold of Christ, this thing torments them so!

We continued this meeting up to the following Sabbath, and appointed a love-feast for Monday, when we would take leave of the people and bid them farewell. At every meeting some were saved, and when we closed on Sunday evening, there were forty-three who had freely given their hearts to Jesus. By this time we had learned to love each other so, that it seemed hard to think of parting. We met once more, and for the last time, on Monday morning; and then the story of love — the love of Jesus — was told again. Oh, that precious hour! Surely the angels looked down upon that company and listened in amazement to the wonderful testimonies that were given in honor of the name of Jesus and His power to save from sin. The shouts of victory went up to heaven from every heart. While the people gathered around the altar, I endeavored to read the ninety-first Psalm.

We left them without a preacher to continue the work thus begun, but the Great Shepherd of the sheep stood forth in the words just being read, and promised to shelter His little flock and hide them under His protecting wings; and while tears flowed freely — tears of holy joy — we bowed once more at the throne of God, and pledged ourselves anew to Him, who had so graciously condescended to bless us, and had washed us in His most precious blood from all our sins. Some who had threatened to stop our work were standing near the door, and looked on and saw how Christians loved each other, and saw how Christians parted; and while the ninety-first Psalm was being read, some of them came up a little closer and were seen weeping. I do not believe the work stopped there. Eternity will reveal the result of that last meeting. Before closing the meeting we organized a holiness band, and a meeting for the promotion of Christian experience in holiness was appointed to be held each week in the church, and Bro. S. was elected leader. We now sang once more, "Praise God from whom all blessings flow," and at the same time, I, with Bro. Haines, shook hands with all that were in the house.

We had taken up no collections, nor was there a word spoken about finances during our stay among the people, either in private or in public; but as we passed out of the church, several brethren and sisters pressed something hard into our hands; and looking at their faces satisfied us that "they gave cheerfully."

How the Lord Sends the Supplies.

I went to my lodging to prepare for departure. The train was to leave for T—— in two hours. While thus engaged I saw Bro. K. coming toward the house in great haste. I went out to meet him, and he, placing a five-dollar bill in my hand, said: "Brother, I had started for home on my wagon; but when I got outside of the town, my good wife asked me whether I had given you some money, 'and I am sure he needs it,' she added. I quickly jumped off the wagon, and here I am, to give this."

The time had come to go to the station to meet the train. On my way there I met several who had waited to give me some money, with some pleasant words each. One little girl came and said: " Bro. K., I have saved thirty cents to buy you one of Sankey's hymn-books, and here it is. I have put my name inside." I could n't thank her in words, but I took her little hand in mine and wept. Was it not one of the Lord's little lambs! Another little girl was at the station waiting to give fifty cents. We met many there who had come out to take a last look at Bro. H. and myself.

Bidding them farewell, the train started off. My satchel looked a little more respectable now, as I thought. Some sister had put in a new shirt, some socks, and handkerchiefs. To be sure I needed such things, and that is why the Lord provided them for me. Bro. H. and I — once more alone — talked over some of the past experiences, and especially about an experience I had in seeing God's protecting hand; when, about the second evening after commencing our work at W——, I had been told that a crowd of young men intended to collect in front of the church to "give me a sound thrashing." After the close of the meeting, on my leaving the church, I had quite forgotten about the matter. The congregation had dispersed, Bro. H. had gone, and I alone remaining behind, as I had intended to have a word with the sexton. While this man was putting out the lights I talked with him. When the last light was extinguished I stepped outside. My eyes met the faces of over a dozen young men, and in a moment I knew what they were about, — but I took the first one by the hand, and so the second, third, and so on, until I had shaken hands with them all, with a pleasant word for each, then a hearty " God bless you all " and a "good night!" I left them, as I noticed, quite confounded. After reaching the corner of the next street, I could not help turning round to have a look at them, when I saw that each had taken a separate road to reach their homes. They felt ashamed of each other. The Lord had put them to shame. Walking through the midst of them, I went my way, unharmed. This, and many other blessings we had, in which we could plainly trace the guiding and protecting hand of the Almighty God. We laid the trophies down at Jesus' feet. (In 1882, while laboring in Chili, South America, I received the *Harvester*. To my great joy I read there that the work at W—— was still going on, and that they had a good preacher. In answer to their prayers, one had been sent soon after we left.)

In T—— we found the home of Bro. R., a Baptist brother, who, after asking us to stop at his house, and offering the church of which he was the pastor, gave us his experience in the following words: —

"I received the blessing of a clean heart two years ago, and ever since I have been filled with God. I preach holiness to my people, for I cannot keep from preaching it, and, the best of all, living it. Now, the day when I received this great blessing of a clean heart, while praising God I fell to the earth and was quite overshadowed with a flood of glory that filled my heart and threatened to overwhelm me. I thought I was lying beneath a large vessel, filled with the new wine of the Gospel, and with my mouth to the faucet, it was turned on, and the contents flowing and flowing, until in the agony of despair, and in vain trying to stop the flow, I managed to cry out, 'Lord, stop, or enlarge my capacity!' I awoke and found that the Lord indeed enlarged my capacity daily, and I never say any more, 'Lord, stop!' I believe," the brother said, in closing, "God can kill us with love."

We opened the church next day for the people, and although there seemed much prejudice against us Methodists, yet the Lord poured out His Spirit and converted several, and sanctified some. We stayed three days in the place. One day we were invited to dine at a Quaker house. Grand old people they were, and wholly consecrated, but a daughter was not. She, however, called me aside, and had an earnest talk with me concerning her eternal welfare. When I had finished she said: "Then I must now give myself to God, and I shall not arise from my knees until I have the definite witness of a clean heart." The result may easily be guessed. After this sister had prayed, she looked steadfastly to heaven, and if it had not been for the tears that flowed down her cheeks, one beholding her might have thought a marble statue was there beside the chair. Then she arose and praised God for the unspeakable gift of "love made perfect."

The last meeting I held in the M. E. Church, the presiding elder being present. I preached from the seventh of Romans. After the sermon, a young man in the congregation arose and confessed that long he had been seeking the light of liberty, and now he had been enabled to see his own heart, and knew what ailed him, and that, by the help of God, he now accepted Christ as his Purifier. The presiding elder arose and said: "I want to warn the members of my church that, while the words of the young man who has preached sound very good, yet I must tell you that he has much perverted the word of God." Then, addressing the young man who had just testified, he said: "You in reality need nothing — you only give way to the enemy too much, making you believe you are not what you ought to be; and if you will consider the matter, you will find that already you are in possession of just that blessing of which the preacher has spoken in his discourse."

This was a very sad interruption of the meeting. We closed in great sorrow, feeling deeply for the poor people and their presiding elder. But how many are there in the church of the same type, not growing, as those always suppose they do, and hindering the church from growing in the grace of knowledge?

Next morning by rail to C——, where they had had a blessed revival a few weeks ago. So we strengthened the brethren during four meetings, and had the joy of seeing some seeking and finding a clean heart.

CHAPTER II.

SUMMER AND HARVEST-TIME REVIVALS.

BRO. HAINES now returned to Indianapolis to remain there, while I, having consecrated my entire time and life to God, laid my plans to strike out in another direction. I felt sorry to leave Bro. H., but it seemed the will of God. I accompanied this dear brother to his home, and before retiring for the night we pledged ourselves to pray for each other always. Lodging at a hotel for that night, before retiring I bowed in prayer, and while praying, I asked the Lord to make me a present of a Bagster's Bible, and I said: "You know, Lord, one of those with flexible covers, references, and a concordance." (Up to date I had been the proprietor of a small ten-cent Testament. I had used it in all my meetings, and it had gotten quite worn. I had seen some of those nice Teachers' Bibles, and my heart coveted one, and I had told the Lord all about it, and had begged Him for the book every night for two months.) I grew quite eloquent in my pleading for the book, and said: "Lord, *now*, give me that Bible."

A REMARKABLE ANSWER TO PRAYER.

Just then I thought a hand reached down to me, and behold! — I saw the precious copy in that hand. Quick as thought I jumped up, and at the same time I received an overwhelming baptism of the Spirit; and looking toward the corner of the room where that shining hand seemed to have disappeared, I clapped my hands, and heard myself saying, in a soft whisper, "I got the book! I got the book!" For hours I could not go to bed, but walking the room, I had but words of praise. "I got the book!" I got the book!" I would now and then exclaim.

When I at last closed my eyes in sleep, my last words were: "I got the book!"

Full of faith and joy I arose the next morning, and I pressed the book to my heart in faith. I felt just as though I had it in my hand, and I found no time to look about me, or to think where it was to come from.

After dressing, I walked toward the home of Bro. H., when I met him in the street on his way to my lodging, as he told me. He looked happy, and I thought the dear brother had something to tell me, and so it was. "Do you know, Bro. K.," he began, "I had a singular experience last night. A man who owed me seven dollars, who had borrowed the amount about two years ago, stopped in at my house and paid the debt. Just imagine my surprise! As I had quite given up the money as lost, the more pleasant seemed the surprise. I looked at the money, and, thanking God for it, I said to myself: "I've been long wanting one of those nice Teachers'

Bibles, with flexible cover, references and concordance; but never could afford to buy one."

"You have got the money now, and you had better get one," I said. (While this brother was thus talking, I nearly burst out with my experience of last night at the hotel, which seemed to correspond exactly with his; but by an effort, I kept silent as yet.)

He continued: "I thus stood and rejoiced in my heart over the fair prospect in view, when suddenly I thought of you and your ten-cent Testament, and that the new Bible belonged to you. I gave it up, and I came to meet you this morning, to take you to the bookstore and get it at once."

By this time my eyes had filled with tears of joy, and my heart was full to overflowing. I took my Bro. H. by the hand, but could not speak for some time, and then I told him my experience of last night.

"Now, let's hurry and get it," was all Bro. H. could say. That is how I got my Bible.

Same day I left for F——. My money would not allow me to go farther. I inquired for the preacher in charge of the Methodist Church. Found he was absent, but the officials opened the church for me, and I preached the same evening to the people, it being Saturday. After service I was asked to stay over the Sabbath and preach. I promised I would.

This pleasant Sabbath morning the Lord blessed us

greatly at the church, An invitation was extended to the people to come to the altar to seek pardon, and purity. The altar was crowded, — not a spot left vacant, — and now all prayed earnestly, according to their several needs. The brother preacher just then returned from an appointment, and hearing that someone was preaching in his church, came to hear; and he heard and saw what God had wrought. Several professed to have obtained salvation, and there was great joy. After the meeting I consulted with the brethren, as to the continuance of the meeting; but the brother in charge thought it would be an unwise proceeding, as it was in the midst of harvest-time. I told them that I could praise God for " harvest-time revivals," — it did not matter at what time poor sinners came to God, He was always willing to accept them. But I could not change their minds.

Now, there prevails a very unhealthy "idea in the churches" about "times and seasons." I don't wish to express my mind just now, but I do think, that when the Lord begins a work, and we see poor perishing souls will cluster around the mercy-seat and seek salvation, no man should undertake to raise his voice and smother the work. How often have opportunities been missed in just that way, and how many souls have gone down to perdition, only God knows. If some brethren have acted according to honest conviction, and walking in the light, it is all well, as far as they are personally concerned; but I cannot help fearing, by judging from the words uttered and the appearance of some of the faces, that sometimes preachers and laymen are touched in their pride, because some one else was said to start the work. And then some do not believe in the doctrine of holiness, as revealed in the Bible and as given in the Methodist Discipline.

A Blind Man with Good Eyes.

Monday morning came, and I concluded to leave for Union City, Ind., but I had not a cent of money for the trip, and so I prayed about it. I was walking up and down in front of my lodging (a brother's house who had kindly invited me to stop with him), when I saw a blind man feeling his way across the street by means of a stick in his hands. I watched the man with some interest and sympathy, and saw how nicely he managed to find the way, although being without a leader. As he passed me, I bade him a "good morning." The man stopped, and turning upon me, reached out his hand, and said: "Oh, is that the young man who preached to us yesterday? I think I recognize your voice." I shook his hand and told him that I was that man. "I am just out looking for you, and I am glad that I have met you," he continued, "and I want to give you some money." Smilingly he went on to say: "I am only a poor man, and I have no money to give; but when I heard this morning that the meetings were not to be continued, I thought of course you would soon leave the place, and while offering my morning prayers, I was much impressed concerning your needs. I did not know how to help you, but I thought to see you at once and hear from your lips something about your affairs." I could see that this dear brother possessed the mind of Christ, and that he had keen spiritual eyesight, "so that the Lord could use him." I then told him that I had just been praying to God to send me on my way, and to provide. The brother said: "I thought as much, and now I will go and get the money." He left, but soon returned with money in his hands, which he had collected from friends who had attended the meeting yesterday. On investigating, I found I had just enough to take me to Union City, and twenty-five cents left.

Now, why was God pleased to use just this poor and blind brother? It is not always the rich whom the Lord can use for such purposes. God, however, is able to save the rich and cause them to give of their wealth; and, thanks be to God! he has those among the rich who will let Him use their money.

The Lord thus proved to me continually that He had engaged to provide for my every need in answer to simple childlike prayer. The arrangement for my supplies was complete when I started on the eighteenth of May. Praise and all glory be to God!

A Wonderful Experience.

The train left F—— late and I arrived in Union City at 11.20 P. M., near midnight. On starting from F—— I had not considered the question as to the time of my arrival in Union City, and had long forgotten the fact that I only possessed twenty-five cents, but I enjoyed perfect rest and looked to the source of all my blessings, and He had promised not to fail me, and trustingly I leaned on Him who has made the world. But few people were in the train, and soon they disappeared to sight, perhaps making their way to a snug little home, or to some fine hotel. Did I envy them? I, the child of a King? Oh, no, no, no! a thousand times, no! With my heart filled with inexpressible joy, I looked up to God and said: "Lord, give me a stone for a pillow, the blue heavens for a covering, the Holy Spirit standing guard, and the world can have the palaces, the ease and comfort; but keep Thou me from sin." But the Lord had a place for me, and in deep humility and in that position, praising and adoring my Master, I desire to note down this wonderful experience which I was now graciously permitted to pass through.

I was walking up some street; I did not know just where I was going to; but thought that somewhere I might discover a light, for no lights were to be seen in this street, and the windows showed no sign that within any one was still awake; only the moon had turned out in full. I had walked, say two or three squares, when I turned up to the left, and approaching the next corner house, I saw a man sitting on some steps that led up to the door of the house, in a half slumber. I stepped up, and touching him on the shoulder, asked him to be kind enough to show me to some lodging-house. The poor fellow was frightened out of his wits, and I thought that moment that I might have been more careful in awakening him. He must have caught only my last words, for jumping up, he stumbled up the few steps and said "Lodging-house, sir? Yes, this is one," at the same time thundering at the door with his fist with all his might. I wished almost I could have prevented him, for really I did not know that I wanted a hotel, remembering that twenty-five cents was all the money I had. Before I was able to say — "Wait a moment!" a voice was heard from within, and at the same time the light of a candle illuminated the window-panes nearest the door. It was too late now, to get out of the dilemma. I could but stand still and see the salvation of the Lord. A peace that passeth knowledge possessed my heart, and I waited. "Who wishes to see me?" I heard a pleasant voice inquire, and the next moment the door was opened, and, what I expected, to judge from the voice I had heard, a rather pleasant-looking man appeared in deepest *negligee* at the door. "Ah, a stranger! Come in, sir, come. Excuse me, sir, for keeping you waiting so long, but I had just dozed off when I heard the knock at the door."

Midnight Grace.

Now I thought the man manifested considerable grace to have so pleasant a face, when called to get up at such an hour of the night; and then to beg to be excused for keeping me so long. I should have begged his pardon for disturbing him; but I had no time to say anything. I only realized a home-like feeling creeping over me, and that my fingers were mechanically rummaging the waist-coat pocket for the twenty-five cents. "Yes, sir, I would like to have a bed for this night, but — but — but — but, — well — " in a faltering voice, I brought out as much as — "got only twen—" I was cut short by the pleasant-looking man, with the words — " Oh, my dear sir, don't mention that now; I will take the light and you just follow me." And my twenty-five cents slid back into my pocket, and before I knew how, we had reached what was to be my bed-room. " Here you can sleep, sir," said the good man, and giving me the lighted candle, pressed my hand and bade me a good-night, and disappeared. For a few moments I stood, motionless in the center of the room; all was so quiet about me; and, as it were, awaking from a dream, I put down my light on the washstand, hid my face in my hands, and wept. How long I stood there I cannot tell. I only know that my eyes fell on a little stand near the bed, and what met my gaze? I was sure I could not be mistaken,—it was a copy of the Bible, *in a hotel!* Oh, that was too much for my poor heart to bear! I pressed the precious book to my heart and sank down upon my knees; but I could not utter a word. I fell flat on the floor, and I lay there long—very long—unable to stir or utter a word. I was lost in God—standing in the cleft of the Rock—Jesus—and beholding the glory of God the Father. I arose and quietly laid down to rest. Scarcely had my head touched the soft pillow, when sleep closed my eyes. I feel utterly unable to enlarge on the foregoing or to express what I felt and my eyes had seen. It passeth understanding. "Praise the Lord, O my soul, and forget not all His benefits!" O that men would trust God, and believe what He says!

The following morning I arose much refreshed, and then I had a sweet hour of conversation with the Father, and Jesus, my Saviour. First, I thanked God that He had led me into the house of a Christian. It was now very plain to me that the proprietor must be a disciple of Jesus. The Bible on the stand in my room, explained much to me. It explained to me the pleasant face of the man, the hearty welcome, and his kindness The words of the Saviour then came to me: "Inasmuch as you have done this unto one of the least of My disciples, you have done it unto Me;" and I asked the Lord to bless the good man of the house.

My plan was now to see, first the preacher in charge of the M. E. Church, for I made it a rule to go to my own people first, and if the doors were closed upon me, I turn to other denominations, preaching the same free Gospel. Passing through the office, I desired, of course, to see the proprietor, and thank him for his kindness, but I found him very busily engaged, talking with some one. Thinking it wise not to disturb him, I stepped out on the street, and bidding him a good morning, said that I would be back shortly to have a talk with him. The man hastily broke his conversation, and, running to stop my progress, he said, "Now, you are not going away without taking your breakfast. Just go down to the basement. There you find the dining-room; sit down, and orders have already been given." That was more than I had anticipated, for I had thought too fast that morning, and, stepping out to go at once to the parsonage, I had quite forgotten that, since 12 M., the previous day, I had taken nothing for the stomach's sake. With thankful heart I sat down to the table, and also asked God to bless the cheerful giver. How desirous I was to see that man, and to speak to him! The dear Lord, however, prevented me that morning, and, simply for the purpose of giving us both a full blessing, as I could see, to my great joy, a few hours later.

My benefactor was still engaged in business, and, as I thought, making out some accounts with the same person that was with him half an hour before. This time I left the house without giving notice, but determined to be back as soon as possible. Some person on the street pointed out to me the parsonage, and soon I was introduced. Bro. M., the pastor, seemed glad that I had come, and gave me the church for services, and any length of time I desired to continue the meetings. Then he gave me the name of a Bro. R., a shoemaker, and said it would be well to see him at once, and get him to make my arrangements concerning invitations, and visiting the people. I started out at once to see Bro. R., and had no trouble in finding him. Everybody seemed to know him. After a hearty greeting and a few words, I thought he might be the sort of man, "known and read of all men," for truly he was one of the Lord's "peculiar ones."

Bro. R. had been praying for some one to come and give a start, for he was one of those who believe in a revival to last 365 days in the year. We soon were ready to start out to visit another brother who kept a livery-stable. When he knew who I was, he said: "Did'nt you stay last night at the hotel of Bro. ——?" I did not know, of course, whether it was the hotel of Bro. —— or not; but I pointed out the place, which I discovered was close by, and the man said, "Yes, that is his place. Well," continued he, "Bro. —— has seen the pastor this morning, and he was told that a young man had just left, who asked to have the church, and that a series of meetings were to be held soon; and by the description of the person, which the pastor gave him, and Bro. —— gave me just ten minutes ago, it must be you, sir. And now Bro. —— is in search for you. He would like very much to see you."

I, of course, understood the whole, and hastened to meet this dear brother. We met, and great was our joy. Bro. —— said that he felt almost certain what I was, after he had taken me to my room last night, for he had seen, while speaking to me, part of my Bible looking out of my overcoat pocket, and he recognized it at once as "the book." He went on to say that he felt blessed all night, and all the morning, and especially, while I ate my breakfast, and that he felt as anxious to see me as I was to see him, only he could not manage to get away from the customer, when he saw me waiting at the door in the morning. We both praised the Lord for His wonderful blessings. His ways are paths of peace and joy. Who would deny it? Though poor, I am rich, and with Habakkuk I rejoicingly say: "Although the fig-tree shall not blossom, neither shall fruit be in the vines; the labor of the olive shall fail, and the fields shall yield no meat; the flock shall be cut off from the fold, and there shall be no herd in the stalls, yet I will rejoice in the Lord, I will joy in the God of my salvation." Amen, even so, Lord.

Doing business for eternity, and investing in it, pays the largest and surest interest, — our eternal weight of glory — a crown that fadeth not away and a home not made with hands, eternal in the heavens, prepared for them that love Him and serve Him in true holiness all the days of their life.

Meetings were begun next day, at 7.30 P. M., and the altar work at once was taken up, and God set His seal to the work, and many were either converted or entirely sanctified. There was a great rattling of dry bones, thank God! and Christ's touch brought life and beauty. Some who had no family prayer, and even feared to ask the blessing of God when at their meals, were enabled to take up their duties. They were members of the church for years, "in good standing."

On the following Sabbath, the pastor himself intended to preach to his congregation, and I accepted a call to preach at Mount Zion Church, about eight miles away. Bro. R. and I walked to our appointment amid rain, the road being very muddy; but we went our way rejoicing. Notwithstanding the unfavorable weather, a good congregation had assembled in the neat little chapel, and three souls were brought to Jesus.

During the following week the meetings were continued in the Union City M. E. Church, under great blessings, and for the following Sabbath I had again accepted an invitation to preach at Raper Chapel, about twelve miles away from Union City. A number of workers from the city accompanied me, and together we bowed before God, entreating Him to give us the fullness of His Spirit for the work before us; and as the disciples of old were waiting before Lord for the baptism of the Holy Ghost, so did we, and experienced the same gracious filling. However, as to the subject for consideration in the service, I was not permitted to see my way clear until just before reaching the house of meeting.

AN EXPERIENCE IN SELECTING A TEXT.

My mind had been much exercised for several hours, and I could obtain no light whatever. I prayed to God with my open Bible before me, but to no effect, but with the exception that at last I arose with quiet peace in my soul, and confidence toward the Saviour, and it was plain that, for once at least, the Lord would give me the word just in time. Walking to the chapel with several of the brethren, not a word was spoken, but just as we were coming up to it, one of the party dropped a word concerning the Lord Jesus, when, clapping my hands, I could not help praising God aloud, and cried: "I have it now: It is finished, it is finished"! And this was my text for that day. Right from the beginning there was a remarkable feeling among the people and an almost anxious looking forward for a great baptism of the Spirit,—and it did come, bursting like a mighty flood upon the whole congregation. I hardly said the last word, when there was a rush for the altar made by those stricken by the word, without waiting for an invitation to come forward. The Spirit of God was at work. Quicker than I take down my notes, thirteen precious souls had fallen prostrate at the feet of Jesus, and many, in tears, were pleading with their God, for Christ's sake to pardon their sins, while others prayed for sanctification by faith, and again others, as they touched with their knees the floor, with bright and shining faces, while yet at the same time tears sparkled in their eyes, praised God at once for the great blessing of cleansing from all indwelling sin, that they just now experienced for themselves.

While I was busily engaged in putting my workers into position, here and there, to assist some struggling souls, I beheld,to my great joy, that all over the church, and in their seats, saints and sinners were on their knees, and one universal cry arose from their lips to heaven: "Lord, save! Lord, save!" It was wonderful; we had a Pentecostal blessing. There was work to do for the brethren and sisters who had come with me from the city, and, thanks be to God! most of them had experienced that the blood of Jesus cleanseth from all sin, and at this altar were enabled to do efficient service for the Master, in pointing out to the seekers of heart purity the way to Jesus. It was a grand sight to see those who had followed their Master faithfully, and according to the light they possessed, through the regeneration. How sweetly these dear souls entered "the valley of blessings." With some there was but little of confession, and but little struggle, — they seemed to drink in the truth; and, looking up to heaven, they simply received Jesus, and said "Lord, now I am wholly Thine." Others, again, found that sin had been indulged, and that forgiveness must first be sought and obtained, and then passed right on to holiness entire. The workers understood their work, and did thorough altar service, which is of so much importance, as many seek the entire sanctification of their hearts, while in reality they need to be reclaimed from a half backslidden state; or some seek to be reclaimed, while they never before have possessed the *knowledge* of sins forgiven. Only those "filled with all the fulness of God," are really fit to do altar or inquiry-room work. How to work with seekers was never before made so plain to me, nor did I ever before feel such a tremendous weight of responsibility resting on me; but, thanks be to God! seeing the light, I was enabled to shift its weight on the Master, and truly the result could be left with the

Mighty to save. This will be a day to be remembered in the history of Raper Chapel.

The work did not close with that Sabbath service, but the holy fire was kindling hearts all over that section of the country round about Union City. Souls were inquiring the way everywhere, and desired meetings in their respective churches.

On returning to the city, I opened meetings at the U. B. church. Pastor A. at first opposed the doctrine of holiness and did so for four or five days, rising at the close of each meeting and saying something to contradict certain things. But on Saturday the Lord gave me a precious text—"Go up and possess the land." God's Holy Spirit was present, and the long-looked-for breaks in the ice seemed to be not far off, and at the close of the sermon the "cracking" could be heard, caused by the pastor of the church himself. He arose and said that he was to preach on the morrow (Sunday) at an outside appointment, and, strange to say, he had chosen the same text, and prepared his sermon; but, he continued, if the interpretation that I had given to the text was correct, then his entire sermon would be spoiled for him; and then he went on to defend his sermon, falling in to the "common error," that the wilderness presented the life of God's people on earth, and "Canaan," heaven; and he intended to encourage his flock to go on as they had hitherto, only, not to be discouraged, but wait till the Master calls them home to enter the valley of blessings so sweet. Sweet, indeed, to listen to, especially to a good speaker, and he would succeed in getting his congregation to shed tears; but, as the preacher disconnects the text from its connectional Scriptural meaning, so thus he leaves his people without the root of the matter, and if by feeling, simply, the poor souls must retain or rather manufacture courage, they will continue to be discouraged, and in the unequal fight with a wilderness experience, fall in the wilderness, their bones bleaching in the sun. Such have just enough religion to make them miserable. Now, up to date, not a soul had come to Jesus. It seemed that the Lord would now begin with the one who stood in the way of the sinner and the thirsting believer; hence, with great joy the angels heard the half confession. But still the cloud hung heavily above us. It caused us to move closer up to the Redeemer, and faith was strengthened. Prayer was soon to be answered, for our dear brother, the pastor. This was the Saturday morning meeting.

How the Lord Slew a Goliath.

In the afternoon meeting the blessing came, but not without one more sore trial for the Lord's people. After I had delivered my message, Bro. A. wished to speak. We were anxiously waiting to hear, and, holding our breath, we all listened. But it was a sad beginning. The poor brother told the people to leave the church, and not come back to hear me any more, as I led the people astray. These were moments of great trial, and if the Lord had not been the General, His children should have been defeated that moment. Turning about while the brother was yet speaking, I said with a loud voice to the workers: "Brethren, pray, and have faith." Hardly had these words been uttered when the pastor turned upon us, and who would imagine what followed now? I arose, and being filled with the Spirit, threw myself on his neck, and weeping bitterly, I cried: "Bro. A., the time has come when God shall open thine eyes and thou shalt see the light." The whole congregation, and all the brethren, were in tears. The salvation of God appeared at that moment, and Bro. A., just as though struck by lightning, fell down at Jesus' feet, and solemnly prayed God to help him — to open his eyes; and give him a clean heart — a heart from sin set free — "a heart in every part renewed — a copy, Lord, of Thine." The lips that had just pronounced the anathema, now were pouring forth praise and blessings upon Him who had this moment done the work. All the workers on their knees about our dear brother, rose up, and while remaining in this position, we praised God with tears in our eyes, and our hearts overflowing for joy; and embracing each other, we arose, greeting each with a holy kiss. Now, all this occurred in the sight of all the people, Some had left their seats, but remained at the door to look on and behold the sight. It was heaven on earth, and " God had come our souls to greet, and glory crowned the mercy-seat."

A man who had much resisted God, had said to Bro. A., when he took the platform to speak, after I had closed : " That's right, Bro. A., now give it to him." He who had thus spoken, ran and left the church when the sudden change took place. So, many flee from God at a time when God would save them, and while they stand and watch and see others actually entering the pearly gates, they turn their backs on the scene, and enter the gates of hell. Is it possible! Oh, poor deluded souls! bewitched by the devil! shake off the viper that has fastened upon thy heart, shake it off into the fire of God's sin-consuming love, and let Him set you free from certain death.

From that day the ice melted away, and a soft breeze from "over the river" began to refresh the faltering ones. The Lion of Judah came to loosen the bands of iniquity, and set the daughter of Zion free, and a mighty shout rose up to heaven from the hearts of scores who were gloriously saved from sin, during the meetings that now followed. When the people on the following day, heard Bro. A.'s message from his own lips, a heartfelt " Amen! " rose up to God.

The following Sabbath the Lord sent us to Rose Hill and was pleased to save five precious souls at our first meeting, and in course of a few days the Lord had called about forty souls, and the dead heard the voice of the Son of God, and His children were in healthy condition to remove the stones, and the called came forth; yea, and parents were enabled to take off the "grave-clothes" that they had put on their children, and there was great joy all over the country. So many invitations came that we had to shape our movements, and begin upon a regular plan of battle. Meetings were arranged for in many different parts of the country, and the fire was burning everywhere round about us. That was now in July.

Filling Out a Number of Blank Checks.

The weather had become quite warm, but I wore still the same suit of clothes that I wore on first setting out in the work, and it was made for winter. Doing considerable "knee work," my pantaloons were worn out at the knees, and quite thin thereabouts. Returning from Rose Hill I discovered a small rent across the knees, and also, that, on the whole, things in general would soon part company. It was the only suit of clothes that were in my possession, and until now had been sufficient. Seeing how matters stood, I made haste through some back streets, till I reached my lodgings, which was at the house of Bro. R., and quickly running up stairs, I bowed my knees once more before the Heavenly Father, and told him all about my pantaloons, and also told him to behold the plight I was in; and I filled a blank check, for a whole suit of clothes. When I arose I knew the Lord had heard me, and hastened down stairs. Bro. R. said to me, stepping into the room, "I have just met Bro. ——, from Mt. Zion. He handed me some money for you, and I've been thinking you need a light coat, and so I went at once to buy some alpaca, and here it is, and my good wife will, with great pleasure, cut the pattern and make it for you at once." And, unrolling the package he carried, I saw some very nice white stuff in the same parcel, and Bro. R., holding it up to me, said: "Now, you see, when I bought the coat, the clerk in the store asked, 'Is this for you, Bro. R.?' 'No,' I said, 'it is for Bro. Krauser.'—'Oh, then he must have a waist-coat, and I'll measure it off, and please accept it as a present.' There was Bro. —— in the store, who overheard our conversation, and stepping up he said, 'If you give Bro. K. a white vest, he ought to have two, to change when the one is in the wash, so please measure off another, and I'll pay for it.' You see, Bro. Krauser," continued Bro. R., "that is the way things come about."

I did not say anything,—my heart was too full. I

bade the good brother good-night, and again worshipping the Lord, I poured out my heart, and felt truly thankful toward Him who had immediately answered my prayer. While I had been praying, the Lord had given orders at once; now I said: "Lord, my pantaloons!"

Meeting Bro. ——'s Sister R. in the morning, I found that this good sister had been working until quite late last night, and had finished the coat, and nearly finished one waist-coat. After breakfast and family prayer, I put on my new coat with thankful heart, and went to the post-office to mail some letters. Passing one of the stores a voice called me back. On turning I recognized dear Bro. ——, who took hold of my hands and said: "Glad to meet you this morning, and while you are handy we can settle the business at once. Bro. Krauser," he said, "I want to make you a present of a good pair of pantaloons. You select the cloth; a tailor has already agreed to make them for you, free of charge, because I have spoken about it already."

Now, what was I to do but to praise the Lord silently in my heart, and do as I was bidden. The following day I was in possession of the clothes; but that same day, in the afternoon, I discovered, to my horror, that the top-leather of one of my boots had split, and the white stocking appeared for same reason to get a peep at the light of the day. It must have just occurred, for all was right a short time before. Well, long enough I had worn them, and why did I not at once include boots in my petition of two days ago, and the thing would not have happened. Looking at my foot in pity, I learned a lesson, and hurried home.

Martin Luther's Ink-bottle. — A Comparison.

I took to the ink-bottle, and tried my skill in painting a certain white spot black. I succeeded pretty well, but in doing this I felt somewhat ashamed for not claiming a complete suit at once, a few days before. But I had not thought. The Lord give me a " clear mind and a large hand," always! However, Satan also tried to have his say while I was "painting," — suppose the ink drew him. "Now, you are nicely treated, — if you go on preaching you'll soon be in rags." As a good Dutchman, I was about to compare Luther's ink-bottle, with the one in my hands; but quickly the thought came that Satan's suggestion was not worth quite so much as to spoil our good brother's papered wall: and, — throwing the black coat straight into his hideous face, it knocked him quite out of my sight.

Crying, " Praise the Lord! " I got my boots, too. I left the house with Bro. R——, and preached that evening again at the —— church, and great blessing attended our efforts.

Now, the next day came a blessing such as often was

my portion, from the hands of my Heavenly Saviour. While up town I saw a wagon coming down the street, and I thought I recognized Bro. C., from Rose Hill,— yes, it was he. Bro. C., who always smiled and shone, and who always had his mouth "full of the Canaan grapes," as he used to say, jumped off the wagon, and we greeted each other with a hearty shake of the hand, and a holy kiss. Then he said: "I have some business to attend to, and if you will accompany me I shall be very glad." I consented, and soon his business was finished. Going up the street he entered a boot and shoe store, and bought a pair of boots for himself; and when he had put them on, he said: "Now, Bro. Krauser, you select a pair for yourself, and accept them as a present from me in the Lord."

Then, soon after, when we were alone, I told Bro. C. my experience, and the prayers, and how God had been pleased to answer these petitions. We long stood and praised the Lord for His wonderful goodness and love towards His children, and the ways He leads those who will trust Him for everything. (Dear Bro. C. is now in South America, preaching and teaching in connection with Bishop Taylor's self-supporting mission. I wonder what he will say when he shall look back on this sweet experience of the past life, and see that the Lord has not forgotten his labors of love. "Praise the Lord!" he will say, while his large blue eyes will fill with tears of joy.)

"Then scatter seeds of kindness,
For the reaping by-and-by."

To none living on earth were intimations of my needs made. The Lord only had been told, and He did answer in His own way. Praise the Lord, O my soul, forever! The flow of supplies did, however, not stop here; but, as with one common consent, the people brought shirts, stockings, handkerchiefs, and such things as I stood in need of.

It was now the ninth of July, and I received an invitation, together with some other brethren, to take charge of a camp-meeting at the W—— grove. The time for separation had come, and I bade my many friends, and those who had so cheerfully helped in the good work, a hasty farewell, such as Bros. Reynolds, Gebbhard, Colburn, Tansey, and others.

No collection had been taken, nor had any person been asked to contribute a mite; but the day when starting for the camp-meeting, I received from several sides gifts in money to go on my way, and it proved just sufficient to take me to the grounds. At B——, in Ohio, stopped a few days, preaching, and on the twenty-fifth the meetings on the camp-ground were begun.

The Lord blessed us much there, but not so many were brought to Jesus as we well might have expected. It seemed that the financial scheme had quite absorbed the attention of those leaders who had called the meeting. There were church debts and preachers' salaries to be considered, and it much hindered the soul-saving work. It was hard work to break through, and all felt it so. Yet the Lord saved some. This meeting closed, and with it my arrangements for the future.

CHAPTER III.

MY FIRST MEETING WITH BISHOP TAYLOR IN 1878. — DAYTON CAMP-MEETING.

I HAD no direct, fixed plans, made beforehand, as I always left open a space for the Spirit to push in His voice; and just before leaving the camp I retired to pray, and while talking with Jesus, it occurred to me to go to the Dayton Camp-meeting, to hear others preach, to strengthen my own heart, and gain experience by seeing others work; and, of course, to do any work the Lord might wish me to do. When this question was settled, I arose, and heard at the same time some one calling out: "The last omnibus to the station!" I ran to the tent, snatched up my satchel, and made for the omnibus, for it had already started, and just as I was jumping up behind, one inside took charge of my satchel, and another person running up to the moving omnibus, pressed something soft into my hand and hurriedly left. The omnibus was soon briskly moving toward the railroad station, about ten miles away, and I soon opened my hand and found that it was a five-dollar bill. Not until now did it occur to me that I had no other money, and that I had jumped on the omnibus without a cent in my pocket to pay my fare, and the fare to Dayton. The Lord evidently knew, and accordingly provided, and what of it if He did choose to provide "just in the nick of time?" My arrangement had been made with God, from the beginning, and it had become natural to me to trust — like breathing the atmosphere; and once clear as to what the Lord wanted me to do, I have often been thus wonderfully led to jump, as it were, at a moment's notice, into the omnibus, the Lord kindly moving it for me, so as to take away even the thought of a doubt — not giving me time except just to take hold, and see the salvation of God. It is hard — I find it so, at least — to explain such experience; but I am entirely at a loss to express it. I only know thus it is, and trusting God, as He has led me to trust Him, is so simple and easy, so natural — it is simply childlike; and when He says Himself, "Take no thought," should I wonder if sometimes the Lord so completely hides me in Himself in such emergencies, and takes away thought for the time being? — and then, in some way, I return to consciousness, and opening my hand, find, as in this case, a five-dollar bill in my hand. It is truly God in us, helping us in every way, to be "kept in perfect peace;" and our minds are "stayed upon Him, because we trust Him." Yes, it seems to be a taking away from the reality outside, for a moment.

The money I had received was *just* sufficient to take

me to Dayton. It was there that I first saw William Taylor. He had recently returned from South America, and he was illustrating his discourse from experiences gained in that country. (I had not heard of this man before; but I listened with great attention to what he had to say, and I thought that he was a remarkable man, but never for a moment did I think of work in other lands.)

The Dayton Camp-meeting was a great blessing to me, and I was privileged to preach several times on holiness, in the tent, and God owned the labors of His servant in a signal manner. Preachers and laymen came to seek the great blessing of sanctification of body and soul. One waiter-boy of seventeen used to stand behind a tree and listen whenever his duties did not call him; " but," said he, on being asked concerning his soul, "I cannot give up the world." One day I called upon the brethren to go apart to some lonely spot, and there pray for that boy. We had prayed for about half an hour, when close behind me a trembling voice was heard to pray: " Lord, have mercy upon me, a sinner!" and soon tears of repentance flowed freely; and as I turned to help the poor struggler, because he could pray no more, whom should I behold but the boy we had been praying for? He was happily converted, and proved to be genuine after.

One pastor came into our little circle, and kneeling

down, he said: "I shall not arise until God has, for Christ's sake, and with His own precious blood, cleansed my heart from all sin, and made me whole." He found peace and cleansing in believing. Then came days of power, and what the dear Lord has done there for the perishing world and lukewarm Christians, can never be told. Only, "Praise God!" can I say, and, lost in astonishment and in admiration of Him who has come to seek and to save that which was lost, I go on my way rejoicing.

A Visit to the Place of My Birth.

When the meeting closed, I made a special request that the Lord might permit me to go to C——, the place of my spiritual birth. I longed to see my old friends, and tell them what the Lord had done for me. "If, Lord, it is Thy will, send me the money to go to C——," were the last words in my prayer. Much assured that the Lord would grant me my petition, I arose and soon met several persons, who, taking leave and bidding me God-speed, pressed each some money into my hands — again the amount necessary to permit me to go to C——; not anything above it.

On the seventh of August I arrived at C——, and then soon met the brother who, under God, together with a good sister, were the instruments in leading me out of darkness into light, and from the power of Satan unto God. Both Bro. W. and Sister J. were so glad to see me, and I was at once introduced to the pastor of N. Chapel, who, for the following Sabbath, engaged me to preach for him.

My text was 1 Cor. iii. 1. Subject: "The carnal mind in believers." After the service had been closed, the dear pastor felt sure that I was altogether wrong in my views on that chapter. I felt exceedingly sorry; but I was as sure as he, and did not change my opinion concerning it. Thus battles were fought and victories won continually; but it always made me feel so heavy when dear Methodist preachers would tell me that they opposed the doctrine of perfect love. They were, as a rule, much older than myself, and so I could only pray God that the time would come when the Methodist clergy would, to say the least, abide by the M. E. Discipline as touching the doctrine of holiness; and God in His mercy would surely lead them to "search the Scriptures," as to whether these things be so, and sanctify and purify them, and endue them with power from on high.

In the evening service this dear brother preached against the theory, and took for a text the words found in 1 Cor. ii. 9, which reads as follows: "Eye hath not seen, nor ear heard, neither have entered into the heart of man, the things which God hath prepared for them that love Him." From such a text to disprove the possibility of the present enjoyment of perfect love, is always a failure; and leaving the church, several dear people came to me and said: "Don't be troubled, dear brother, we also feel sorry that our dear pastor kept the *cream*, and gave us skim-milk, for he left out the precious word of the following verse (v. 10), 'But God *hath* revealed them unto us by His Spirit.' We will pray for him," continued the brethren.

Was not this a noble Christian spirit? Yes, pray for him. If it was not for such within the church who see better than their pastor, many a church would have been closed up and sold by auction in the different parts of the vineyard. They resolved to stand by this pastor and pray. That was a good resolution. Amen! So may all do for the pastor who is not yet in the light of holiness. Many souls are being cheated by getting chaff instead of wheat. The Lord save His people, and give power to His saints to tell the story of complete deliverance, that others may hear and be glad.

Bro. W. then invited me to attend the L—— Camp-meeting, which I did,

His Grace All-Sufficient.

The Lord there saw fit to permit a great trial to befall me, which in the end proved to be a good, which God intended for me. I had taken some meals with Bro. W. in a tent which was occupied by another Christian family. One day I was not called to take my dinner, but the good brother came out to me, and, handing me fifty cents, told me to go to the boarding-tent and get a meal there. He looked sad and he saw that I had noticed it, and before I asked a question, the brother took me aside and said: "The children of that family in the tent refuse to eat with you at the same table, because they knew you before your conversion to have been a great sinner."

I begged dear Bro. W. to leave me for a time. I desired to be alone. It was all that I could say. On what now passed between me and my God, I will draw a curtain, and say only this: I wept bitterly, oh, how bitterly! My past life rose up before me, and the sins of that life rose up once more to my vision as in the days when I repented, some years ago. My heart bled, and I cried to God to keep me in perfect peace, and to give me a glorious victory. Yes, it was a victory beyond description. There was no feeling of ill-will toward those who refused to eat with me. Yes, I felt that I was the unworthiest of creatures, but through the precious blood of Jesus, made the child of a King, and made to sit down in heavenly places. The hand of Jesus raised me up from my knees, and such sweet peace and joy entered my heart! oh, so sweet and so comforting, that I was lost in wonder, and thanked God for the trial. It humbled me anew before God, and He enabled me to see, through the dark cloud, the lesson, how good it is to be humbled at times, when we are in the midst of successful Christian work, and winning victories for Jesus on all sides. Oh, how I feel to thank the blessed Jesus for His goodness to me! Only one question arose in my mind which made me sad again. It was, Are those poor souls in that tent the Lord's beloved? I trust and pray we may one day meet in heaven around God's white throne, and meet as those who have come up out of great tribulation, and washed our robes white in the blood of the Lamb.

The Lord had much work for me in other parts of the camp-ground, and when on the following day I was hungry, I prayed to God for food, and, walking through the thousands of visitors, I cast my eyes for a moment to the ground, and just then I saw something glittering in the sun, and stooping down, I held in my hand a twenty-five cent piece. This was invested in food, and it being near the close of the meeting, I took leave of Bro. W. and walked to an Allbright camp-meeting. I desired to get acquainted with them. It was a days' journey from L——, but I had just prayed the Lord to give me a pleasant journey, when a buggy passed by, and a pleasant-looking man asked me whether I wished to have a ride. Consent was given, and I found the man was not a Christian. When I told him how I had just been praying while walking along the road, the man was much affected, and expressed a desire to become a Christian. We rode together for some hours, and the Lord had a word for this man's soul. I trust to meet him in heaven.

I soon was at the camp-ground, and the man with whom I rode had taken another road. I was well received by some of the brethren, but found the "cloth had been cut already." The time was taken up by workers of their own denomination, and no chance given me to preach. However, the Lord used me the following day to work at the altar. The day after I left the camp-ground, and making my way to the nearest railroad station, I there met Bro. W., of C——, who paid my passage to C——. Stopping there the second time, the Lord added many souls to His church.

On the 25th of August I received a note to go to S——, Bro. Birdsall's charge, to hold meetings there for the promotion of holiness, together with some other brother of the Ohio Holiness Alliance. Bro. B. had just accepted a call to South America, to the Isthmus, to work under William Taylor.

I there heard more about Taylor's work, and one day Bro. B. asked me plainly: "Would you go to South America if you were called?"—"If called of God, I should obey," was my answer, "but as yet I do not know of such a call." The matter was dropped, and the meetings continued for some days. The Lord converted and sanctified a few, and the hours with Bro. Birdsall and his good wife were seasons of great blessing. (Bro. B. went to the Isthmus of Panama. He was the first missionary that was sent to South America by William Taylor. He worked too hard, and God took him after he had been with his flock but a few months.)

On the 4th of September there was a camp-meeting at M——, which I attended, and the Lord used me there in various ways to lead seekers to Jesus, and give testimony for Him in the different meetings.

Struck in the Face.— Glory and Praise.

While there, a woman who had been mightily convicted of sin, came to me after the meeting and said: "Sir, I saw you looking at me in the hall, and I wanted to know whether you meant me with what you said, when you were preaching. Do you mean me, sir, or not?" — "My dear woman, I do not know you — never met you before, but if you are 'hit' I dare say the Lord intended His message for you, for, indeed, I preached to the unsaved, and surely meant them in particular who still live in sin."

At this explanation the poor woman became quite angry, and before I knew it she had struck me with her fist. I threw up my hands, and clapping them, I shouted: "Glory to God! Glory to God!" and was, in the twinkling of an eye, so filled with joy that for a time I forgot my surroundings. When I looked about me again I saw some of the brethren standing near, but the woman was gone. Poor thing! got scared, no doubt; perhaps she expected a fight, and in that case I believe she would have stood like a man, for she looked quite determined to make me answer; but this was, evidently, too much for her —she could not stand when God was speaking. Poor soul: I was blessed and she was not. God be praised for a living Jesus within the soul.

In a Prison.

Towards the end of the meeting, out at the camp, the Lord called me to visit the county prison. Some sisters accompanied me, and God was with us in great power. From cell to cell we went and invited the poor captives out into the court-yard to hear the preaching of God's word. Some excused themselves, saying they needed nothing. Quite innocent, I presumed. Others were playing cards, others reading,—however, some came out to hear us. While yet speaking I saw a tall, strongly-built man, leaning his forehead against the iron bars of a window, and soon I saw how hard he tried to conceal his features, for the tears were trickling down his cheeks, and wet the dingy pavement at his feet. When the meeting closed, and a sister offered the last prayer, loud sobs were heard to proceed from the quarter where the man stood. I walked up to him, but he did not look up — he wept. Then, placing my hand on his shoulder and trying to look into his eyes, he said: "Oh, do not look at me! I am a poor, lost sinner." Then I told him that he was just the man whom Jesus came to save. His looks changed, and the poor man looked at me and exclaimed: "Oh, is this true? Do you think God would have mercy on me now, while I am in prison?" — "Sin has brought you to this place, and God alone is able to bring you out of Satan's prison, and if you truly repent and believe the record that God gives concerning His Son, and make an unreserved surrender of yourself to Him, He is willing to save you this moment."

The man sank down upon his knees, and then, before we left the prison, was made to rejoice in the Saviour. (Just before leaving the country I received a letter from this man, in which he states that he had soon been discharged from prison, and obtained employment, and that he had connected himself with the church.)

After once more preaching to the people at M——, on the public square, from an old shoe-box, I received another call to go to Union City and Rose Hill. The work about there had been continued after my departure, and the brethren wanted help for a season, for God had prepared the field. In the morning of the next day I attended the closing of a meeting, when I felt I must be going, if the train should not start without me.

The brethren knew about my going, and so I arose from my knees during prayer offered by several workers, and on tip-toe, made my way through those kneeling about me. One sister seeing me go, took hold of my hand, and pressed a few bright dollars into it, and without rising from her knees or saying a word, we parted, and soon I sat in the cars. This sister had given me enough to pay my passage to Union City. Now, Lord, just in good time! I had no money when I rose from prayer, but I had had a talk just then with Jesus, and I knew in some way He would provide; however, I never thought it would come from any one engaged in prayer, and while kneeling; but our thoughts are surely not God's thoughts in such things, and He often, in a most pleasant way, shames us if we have had any thoughts about the "how."

The joy of meeting the loved ones once more, was great, and "to work," was the word again. To relate the experiences of this second campaign, is quite beyond possibility. If we had blessings before, they came in greater power this time, and soon the Lord had thirty souls saved at Rose Hill, and five more in one day's meeting at Mount Zion Church.

Justification and Sanctification Inside of Fifteen Minutes.

Here is the experience of a dear sister. For several

days she had come to the altar, but could find no peace. When the meetings were closed at Rose Hill, she followed to a chapel some five miles distant. When there the altar was crowded with seekers, and she was one of them. But there she was enabled to make a full surrender of herself to God, and was caused to rejoice exceedingly. Speaking with her, I found her very clear, and her testimony was the "shibboleth" unmistakably correct. Passing on to other seekers, and helping as far as I could, together with other workers, my attention was soon called to the other end of the bench, and I saw the sister just spoken of, in deep thought, her head hung upon her hands; she was evidently troubled. Thinking that the enemy was trying to get the poor sister to doubt her acceptance, I bowed down and asked, "Sister, what is it you are thinking about?" Looking up, she said, solemnly: "Bro. K., you have been preaching holiness, and I have heard you so often; and the Lord has just now been showing me, while here, the distinction between sins forgiven and sins cleansed, and it corresponds with my inner condition; and knowing positively my sins forgiven, I now desire the cleansing from all indwelling corruption. I see it clearly, dear brother, and now tell me, can I not receive it now?" and with tearful eyes she watched my reply.

"Yes, God will do all He has engaged Himself to do for us, according to His promise. Ask and you shall receive, and — the blood of Jesus cleanseth from all sin."

This being the first case of the kind in my experience with seekers, I looked forward with some curiosity as to the outcome of this before me. I desired to see the salvation of the Lord, and accordingly said but little. However, there was no doubt raised with my feelings, and soon we all beheld what God could do for the hungry soul. God came to bless that sister. There was not that outward manifestation of great joy, as witnessed fifteen minutes ago, when this sister received the knowledge of sins forgiven; but a deep peace took possession of her soul, and scarcely above a whisper she was heard to say, "Now the Lord also sanctifieth me wholly: His blood cleanseth me from all sin. Thanks be to God for a pure heart!" Then, after a time, she broke out in tears of joy, and praised God with a loud voice.

Now I believe this is God's intention, to first pardon and then cleanse; and let no man set space of time, for God can and will save, if but the teaching on those subjects be clear, and sinners receive both doctrines from the pulpit, and are properly assisted when seeking the Lord. Truly hath the Lord showed us His glory and His power to save.

In March, 1879, when laboring in South America, I received a copy of the *Harvester*, where a Bro. W., who was present at that meeting, made the same statements as above to that paper, and adds the following: " Here we have justification and sanctification both, inside of fifteen minutes. A short *growth*, is it not? This winter this sister had bleeding of the lungs. While at her home I saw on one side of her bed, two sick children, while on the other lay the mother, gasping for breath. Her lungs were fast filling with blood, and in a short time she could not breathe, and it took two of us to hold her. She finally sank back upon her pillow, and while we knelt in prayer, I could hear her clap those feeble hands and whisper: 'Jesus! Jesus! Jesus!' On a similar occasion she was alone with a young lady, who ran out of doors. When the struggling could be heard no more, the young lady entered, supposing to find the sufferer dead; but in astonishment found her alive. She asked her: 'Were you not afraid to die?' To this Sister C. replied: 'No, to die is gain for me. Glory to God!' Truly a holiness testimony. Amen."

At the Dayton Camp-meeting, I met a woman who told me she had the blessing of holiness as revealed in the Bible at the moment of conversion; but this good woman at times got so angry that some thought she needed her sins forgiven; and then she contended that everybody gets angry, making it appear as though the Lord leaves at least that much of the carnal mind to trouble us. Now, thus to fight, and struggle, and live, some think to be the "Christian warfare," confounding it with Paul's fight, "fight the good fight of faith." Thank God! He can take away anger, and, under all circumstances under heaven, keep us saved, through the mighty baptism of perfect love. But it is a great pity that so many, like the son in the parable, instead of believing the word of the Father — "Son, *all* that I have is thine," — and taking it, they go out into the barn or pig-sty, pouting it out. Well, those who go in with the Father see how prodigals are brought home, and enjoy the feast. John was of the kind filled with love, and thus was blessed in bringing souls to Jesus, and seeing the wanderers' home, and then he could say: "I have no greater joy than to see my children walk in the truth."

CHAPTER IV.

MY CALL TO SOUTH AMERICA.—A LETTER FROM WILLIAM TAYLOR.

October, 1878.—I was just about to make arrangement for other meetings, for a Bro. C. sent me word to take charge of a ten-days' meeting, and a German pastor asked me to preach in his church. For some time it had been my wish to preach in my native tongue, and I often wondered why it was that the Lord never opened the way for me to enter the German work; but as it was, I had never yet preached in German, and for that reason my answer to this pastor was: "God willing, I shall come." To Bro. C. I wrote the same: "God willing, I shall come." But the Lord had made other arrangements for me. I was just making preparations to attend the calls I had received, when, to my great surprise, I received a letter from the Rev. Wm. Taylor. The letter was read with the greatest care — read and re-read. I could hardly believe my eyes. The letter was very short, and in substance contained the following:—

TORONTO, CANADA, Oct. 27.

Dear Bro. Barchwitz-Krauser,—The other day I sent the Rev. Mr. Birdsall to Aspinwall. He told me something about you, and after praying about the matter, I was satisfied that you are my man.

The Lord wants you to go to South America in my self-supporting missions, and preach on faith line to the Germans in the south of Chili, your own country people. Are you ordained an elder, or local preacher in the church? Write.

Yours in Christ,
WM. TAYLOR.

I at once suspended my preparations to go to my appointments and gave myself to prayer for several days,—prayer and fasting. It came so suddenly upon me—so unexpectedly—that I did not know how to look upon or to face the question; but the Lord helped me. The brethren were consulted, praying much over it. Had the Lord been preparing me for the self-supporting missions of William Taylor? The question came to me again and again. Does God want me to go? By prayer and fasting and waiting for God to speak to my soul, I received, after a hard struggle, a definite answer, and I believe that God had been preparing me for Taylor's self-supporting mission all the time, and I knew God wanted me to go. I wrote only a few lines to William Taylor, saying:—

Dear Bro. Taylor,—I have prayed to God, and it is clear the Lord wants me to go. I say from the bottom of my heart, "Here, Lord, am I: send me."

In a few days an answer came, and Bro. Taylor asked: "Do you need money to go to New York? You must be there in November. Steamer *Acapulco* leaves the latter part of that month."

I wrote back: "(D. V.) shall be in New York in time. Don't want you to send me any money. I had better keep on the self-supporting line, and pray God for the means to go, and accept it of Him as another token of His favor. I am a local preacher in the M. E. Church."

A Visit from William Taylor.

Soon another letter came to my hands, from William Taylor, stating that he was on a hasty trip to Indianapolis, and would cut across to Union City, and there would wish to see me personally. The appointed time came, and Father Taylor emerged from the car. I knew him because of seeing him at the Dayton camp-meeting, and so stepped up at once and took his hand. Father T. looked at me for a moment, and kissed me. "So you are my Dutchman?" he said. "And a child of the King," was my answer.

Father Taylor was taken up to the house of one of the brethren, where he stopped over night. The time was spent in much useful conversation concerning South America. We also had much singing and prayer. The following morning, this, as I thought, remarkable man, took his departure.

There was something in all his movements and manners, and in all he said or sang, that impressed me deeply, and something I had not noticed in any body else; and yet he seemed so humble and childlike, though possessed with a certain grandeur becoming to royalty, — becoming to a son "of the man who made the world," as he used to say. To say it: I fell in love with Father Taylor.

Now, when this thing was noised abroad, I received letters from many friends, with words of encouragement, and many gifts were sent to me, of such things as I needed, such as articles for wear. One good sister made me a present of something very useful. It consisted of different kinds of thread, needles, pins, and buttons, and a neat cloth case, containing the whole. How the Lord blessed me in sending me these tokens of Christian love! Also, I received sufficient money to take me to New York, and on my arrival there had something left. The parting was very affecting; but the light of the Spirit dispersed the gloom. On my arrival in New York, I found a letter addressed to me, which read as follows, in substance: —

Dear Sir and Brother, — Understanding, through the periodicals, that the Rev. William Taylor has engaged you to go to South America, and presuming that no provision has been made to pay your passage, I herewith enclose check for $333. I should be glad to hear from you at any time.

Indiana.
Yours in Christ,
D. P.

Father Taylor did not tell me how I would get my passage to South America, but he said that very probably I should find some letter of further instruction at

805 Broadway, New York; and reading the foregoing letter, it is plain that Bro. T. did not know who was to be the instrument in God's hand to send the passage money; and that when he engaged me, he had not the money in hand, no transit fund being in existence yet.

Thus God prepared and called me to go to South America, under Bishop Taylor.

While waiting in New York, I had the privilege of preaching in some of the churches, in the pulpits and class-rooms, and also to labor at the altar during meetings held by Mrs. VanCott, who was in New York at the time. There I was kept busily engaged up to the last evening before steamer sailing, I also received another letter from Father Taylor, in which he informs me that Mr. Henry Hoffman, of Berea, Ohio, and wife, were to go by same steamer to South America, and enter the German work,—they to work in the Province of Llanquihue, and I to the City of Valdivia.

Leaving for South America.

The day for departure arrived, and Bro. Hoffman and wife came on board. Many friends came to see us off. Thus we embarked on board the *Acapulco*, on the 30th November, 1878, and as the steamer left the pier, we all sang, "I've reached the land of corn and wine." We went to preach a full Gospel to the people of South America.

The first three days out we encountered a terrific storm, and it was a grand sight to us. The mighty waves rose like mountains about us and beneath us, lifting the ship and tossing her, for a few moments, as it were, into the air, which caused her to tremble like a leaf; but then she gracefully sunk down into the valley of the raging ocean, and then it would seem for a moment as if the mountains of water above us had combined to swallow up the ship and her living freight. But we were safe, and without fear we beheld the grand sight. Now and then a huge wave would sweep the decks. At such times we were out of harm's way. The captain understood the weather, and by his orders we had then to remain below. Then came the fine weather, and warm, and just the day before anchoring in the harbor of Colon, the captain of our steamer permitted us to see a sight which greatly contributed to our confidence in him. The fire-bell was rung, and in a few minutes every man of the crew was at his post. Then we saw, when these exercises were over, how the captain slyly cut one of the life-buoys, fastened to the railing, and the signal followed: "Man overboard!" Now followed the spectacle that was so interesting. In a surprisingly short time, one of the boats was lowered and manned, and shot out after the buoy, floating near the steamer, and as quickly brought it on board. This was done in such a short time, that all on board felt satisfied it would not have given time to a person falling overboard to drown. So much for this captain and his crew,—and how about the Captain of our salvation—Jesus Christ? Surely, He is not only willing to save, but He is ready, with His own hands, to save those who, without His saving presence, go down to the bottom of the sea of sin, into which so many of the victims have plunged, and, aside from Jesus, have no rope thrown to them, and see no rescuing boat nearing to save. And yet, outside of Christ, men and women sink, daily, into hell, for they will not call upon Jesus to save them.

The following day we stepped on shore at Aspinwall — a dreadfully filthy place — built up in a swamp, breaking out in fevers; and here we met the Rev. Bro. Birdsall, Bro. Taylor's first man in South America. We found him very happy, and in good health. Our steamer did not make connection at that time with the one on the Pacific side of the ocean, and we were compelled to stop in Aspinwall for about six days.

Our First Revival in South America.

Bro. Birdsall suggested that we have a revival of the Lord's work in that place, and set out at once to invite the people. Bro. H. and myself responded with a hearty amen, and the meetings were begun in the church at once. Every evening we gathered a good congregation, and the Lord graciously poured out the Holy Ghost, and daily many precious souls were soundly converted to God, and many among the believers sanctified wholly, and cleansed from inbred sin. These were days of refreshing among the whites and among the natives, both; and we had no room to regret that we were delayed on the Isthmus of Panama.

The last day in Aspinwall, as we walked down to the train that should take us to Panama, we saw a number of colored men and women, who stood in the streets, and, with a loud voice, praised the Lord for salvation found. They were so filled that it was impossible for them to keep still. Our hearts were filled with thanksgiving, and we had every reason to believe that good numbers had been converted to God, and that one day we shall strike hands with scores of such who found the Saviour during our stay in Colon, when we reach the last outpost, and see each other face to face around the throne of God on high. It was my special privilege to often go apart with dear Bro. Birdsall and talk with him over the deep things of God. He loved so much to talk of those things that pertained to the teaching of holiness — holy living. These hours have been the sweetest of my life, and I think I can never forget Bro. B.'s face, when, after having bathed together in the sunshine of God's marvellous truth, — as it was revealed to us while talking, — when in low strains he would begin to sing the sweet "Beulah hymn," his favorite, and then I would chime in. Next I would take his hand, and, looking at him, would see the tears of joy steal to his eye.

Dear Bro. Birdsall! he has gone home to heaven since. Only a few weeks after I had left him, God took him home. When I read the notice, I could understand it all. I could now understand why he was thus talking and singing with me, and why he seemed so heavenly to me during such hours. God was preparing one of His saints to step into the chariot of fire. Glory to God! Doubly sweet is the remembrance of those blessed hours to me to-day. How can I forget them now? They shall rise up before me when I shall hear the wheels of the chariot of fire. When I hear the tramping of Israel's steeds, I want to think of those hours, — yes, and of the hours we had spent together in his charge, before he left the United States. Oh, how to-day I remember every word that ever passed between us! It is wonderful, and I pray that God may grant me grace to always commune with those about me as in the face of eternity. My friend! my brother! thou hast passed away. Oh, how my heart bled when I heard of it! I hurried into the forest, to a beautiful spot overlooking a beautiful lake, with two snow-capped volcanoes standing with their feet in the lake, just opposite from where I knelt in prayer. There was the beautiful sunshine, and not a ripple on the water before me. Never did the panorama seem so grand! And as, with tearful eyes, I looked up to God, I sang the verses we had so often sung together, —

> "I look away, across the sea,
>   Where mansions are prepared for me."

All was so quiet about me — only the sweet warbling of some birds in the distance; but it seemed as if the great angelic choir joined with me in the sweet refrain. My brother! my dearly beloved brother Birdsall! soon — soon — I shall meet you there, with Jesus and all His loved ones. Glory to God in the highest!

Bro. Birdsall found a fine church-building at Colon, put up by the railroad company, and was permitted to use it for any religious services he might desire. His salary was made up by voluntary contribution by those living in the country, and not from the people or any society at home; and I was expected to live the same way. Bro. B. told me that he received all the money necessary to carry on the work, and that they had no lack. Praise the Lord! He not only preached in the city — Colon — but there was a negro settlement a few few miles to the southwest — Monkey Hill — which he visited regularly every Sunday. I preached once there, and had then several conversions. The people loved Bro. Birdsall, and he had conversions constantly.

Life on the Isthmus.

A great deal of money seems to flow into this port, as also at Panama; and, accordingly, a great deal of vice is visible. Gambling is a prominent feature in those two places, and notwithstanding the bad climate, there is careless living noticeable, among foreigners especially, and the death-rate among them astonished me. I spoke to several who evidently enjoyed good health, and indeed had not been sick with the fever yet, although living on the Isthmus for two or three years. I took notice of what they told me about their mode of living. In the first place they rejected the idea that with every drink of water, brandy or whiskey or wine must be used, because the water is bad; but they took good care that the water they drank had first been boiled, and drank it either pure, or in the shape of coffee or tea, either hot or cold. They thought that people who complained about the bad water, drank too little of it. Second, these wise people thought it to be of great importance to retire early, and have no "late nights," under any circumstances whatever, and eat moderately, and plenty of fruit early in the morning. I thought this explanation to be very reasonable, and am inclined to believe that this is the right mode of living in all such climates. Our good missionary brethren might learn from it, and I expect to take it to heart for my own benefit. One more point seemed clear to me, — such was the moral condition of the people here, that no one man or woman seemed to be free from the danger of being slandered. Purity of life seems to be regarded as impossible on the Isthmus, and any one pretending to it is an object of ridicule. It may then be considered a hard field for a missionary, as the people seem not to hesitate to fling dirt on even a representative of the Church of the living God. Now Bro. Birdsall was married, and a peculiarly fit man for such a field; with a sweet, amiable temper. I don't think I ever heard Bro. B. shout, or manifest much by outward demonstrations; but I could read the joy of his soul in every feature of his face and every look of his eye, and so no doubt could others. The enemies of the Cross of course tried their hand; but they could always behold with their own eyes that the dirt thrown fell off. It did not stick. On the whole, it seemed to me that only the most holy, God-fearing man, would and ought to work here, and that it certainly required great wisdom to work in this field. And not only so, but that in regard to the climate the same wisdom must be used in order to properly divide the time for work, or many precious lives may be sacrificed, and comparatively little accomplished. Now, those people who have followed secular business, and have lived here for two or three years, find it absolutely necessary to change climate for, say two months, every year. By as little work as possible, and very careful living, as above described, the wear and tear of the system is very great. Now, would it not be wise for missionaries and societies sending out men into this field, to remember this? I do not know whether it is wise, under our self-supporting plans, to occupy such a field, where we shall probably be compelled to bring a missionary home once every year; or, in many cases of sickness or death, to renew the outlay for passage money, which might be used to send men and women to other more healthy parts of South America, where workers are so much needed; yet, when I look at the wretchedness and the sinful condition of those residing here, I am asking myself the question, How can we give up the field? It should be cared for. Am I prepared to say, It falls to the lot of the "Taylor Mission"? May God in His love spare our man, and our men, who should be called to labor here?

The trip across the Isthmus was delightful. The train proceeding comparatively slow, I was enabled to take in the beautiful scenery that presented itself to my wondering eyes, and nature-loving heart. The vegetation in this region is something wonderful. However, the low parts, consisting of marshy swamps, have a somewhat melancholy aspect. One would naturally think of the hundreds who lost their lives in building this road through this beautiful-looking country, and think of the poisonous atmosphere of this region, which otherwise would be a Paradise. So I seemed to be enjoying it while passing by, without a desire to even linger for a while. Something wanting.

On the Great Pacific.

Of Panama I saw nothing. I hurried on to the wharf, where the steam-tug was waiting to receive passengers, and to take us on board the *Oroya*, for the South Pacific. The captain we found to be a very pleasant man, an American. Capt. Hall was the only American in the employ of the Pacific Steam Navigation Company, and was the commodore of the fleet of that company, which consisted of about eighty steamers. We were well cared for. Being deck passengers, we put up a sort of tent on deck, the captain kindly furnishing us with the necessary canvas for that purpose. The weather was quite warm, and we enjoyed the trip to Callao, Peru, exceedingly. The beauty of the entrance of the Guayaquil River, and all the way up to the city, — was delightful, and I thought it surpassed anything that I had ever seen before. There was not a ripple on the waters of the wide bay at the entrance of the river, and not a breeze stirred the air; and as the eye would pass over the soft surface of the waters, I could see, now and then, large pelicans plunge from a height into the water about the ship, and in the distance, catching fish, in which they succeeded admirably. Then, as the ship took her course toward the city, the shores on either side drew nearer, and sometimes we would run so close to the banks of the river, that by some effort one might leap on shore. Both sides of the river are lined with beautiful meadows and well-stocked farms. Large orange orchards appeared, and trees covered with beautiful blossoms, and flowers of many colors. The cattle seemed very small, but well fed. Guayaquil is considered very unhealthy during the rainy season, but the interior is not only naturally grand, but also very healthy. We stopped only a few hours in the harbor, and then, being once more privileged to watch the scenes described fade out of sight, we soon reached Callao.

The coast south of Guayaquil presented a very sad face, — not a shrub; nothing of all that gladdened our hearts in the way of scenery which we were accustomed to see almost anywhere where I had been travelling before. A great desert of sand, stretching from here, all the way down to Callao, and farther south, as far as Valparaiso, and even a little south of that city. Leaving Callao we reached Mollenda. There I visited the Rev. Magnus Smith and wife, two of William Taylor's people who had arrived there only a short time ago, and had not yet gotten fairly under way. At Iquique we found the Rev. John Collyer, who had just opened a school, and also preached on Sundays to the English residents. He was getting along well. "Plentiful," Bro. C. said, was the support he received financially, but the place was a hotbed of sin. "Drink is the general crime in this city," he said, "but by the help of God we will go on." His sister was on board with us as a cabin passenger. She had come out to help her brother in the work.

Next we met Rev. Bro. Higgins at Coquimbo, doing a good work there, and travelling several circuits.

The First Money Earned in Chili.

Bro. Hoffman and myself received there from Bro. Higgins the first money earned by him on South American soil. Bro. Higgins said: "Take that — you will need it down South. The Lord provides us here with all I need, and," and, added he, "if only the people would be as willing to give their hearts to Christ as they are to give their money! But," he said, he had had "a number of conversions, and a splendid Sunday-school."

I was pleased to find our dear people so bright-looking and courageous. Several of the workers were stationed in inland towns, and these, of course, I could not see, — such as Rev. J. P. Gilliland and wife, at the Lobos Islands, among the shipping; Prof. Humphrey and wife at Tacna, and Rev. L. Smith and wife at Copiapo. All these, however, I heard were doing well, and being entirely supported by the people among whom they labored. These reports, together with what I was able to see of the workers and the people, encouraged me very much, and my heart rejoiced to know that thus God was dealing with His missionaries.

Bro. Smith Preaches to the Natives.

Bro. Smith, of Copiapo, I was told, although then only a few months in this country, was already preaching to the natives; first writing his sermons and then reading them to his congregation, and he expected in a few months more to so master the language as to be able to take up that work in earnest, and establish a church. Amen and glory to God! I would say from the heart. God bless the dear brethren in that great desert of Atacama, and make it a spiritual Eden.

Much strengthened in spirit and body, I arrived in Valparaiso, on the fifth of January, 1879, where I had to lay over for another steamer to take me to my field, a few hundred miles further south, near the borders of Patagonia, where are several large German colonies. While waiting in Valparaiso, I was invited by Dr. T., of the Union Church, to preach on Sunday evening. The doctor has a fine church, and the better class of the foreign population are his principal supporters. He has been working here for the last thirty-five years, and working much to distribute Spanish tracts and Bibles among the natives, to which end, also, a Bible Society has been called into life, which does great good all over the land. I also found a Presbyterian brother laboring among the natives exclusively, in school work and direct Gospel work. This brother had a short time ago bought the German church, which was sold by them to "quit the business," with hymn-books, etc.

While I preached at the doctor's church, Bro. Hoffmann had invited the Germans to hear him. I understand they turned out well, and it appeared that they only desired a godly preacher, and the work might be taken up again and carried to success.

CHAPTER V.

ON THE BORDERS OF NORTHERN PATAGONIA.

Our orders were to go to the south, and accordingly we prepared for the start. Before starting, however, we learned that the Gustav-Adolph Society, of Germany, had taken up the field south, and had sent two ministers, one to Osorno and the other to Puerto Montt, supplying at the same time a colony of a hundred families, living at the Lake Llanquihue, situated about twelve miles inland, north of Puerto Montt. This somewhat perplexed us, and we changed our plans for operation somewhat, and we thought it wise, as Valdivia, a German settlement of about three thousand persons, alone was left unprovided, and Bro. Hoffmann, being a married man, should go to that city instead of myself, and I to proceed to the province of Llanquihue, and, if possible, make arrangements with the Lutheran pastor in charge of the Lake district, that I might take up that work at the Lake, which I thought quite enough work for one man, if he wishes to do his duty.

The day for departure drew near, and we embarked for Valdivia and Puerto Montt. Valdivia had been described to me as a modern Sodom and Gomorrah.

Thirty years ago this colony had been founded, and never, since that time, had they agreed to any arrangement to have the Gospel preached to them, and in these latter years expressed themselves to this effect, that they were glad to be without a preacher, as the cities of Osorno and Puerto Montt stood for a warning to them, because of the contention and strife among the people since the pastor from Germany had come to these settlements. I do not know how far true this is. Since laboring here, I am sorry to say, the people of Valdivia are not so much to be blamed for this excuse on these grounds. The people of Valdivia did not even get their children baptized, with the exception of a very few families, who had sent to Osorno, the place nearest them, to have the ordinance performed. Osorno can be reached from Valdivia in two days, on horseback.

To this field Bro. H. decided to go, and there to pitch his tent. Bro. Hoffmann is a precious brother, and full of faith and the Holy Ghost. Praise the Lord! I never saw Bro. H. when he did not sing or praise the Lord with all his heart, and *from* the heart, and very seldom when he did not have a soul either by the hand or kneeling on the floor; and I felt that if any man would be blessed of God, it might be he. We separated at Valdivia — " the city of lager beer " – . the Vanity Fair of Bunyan's Pilgrim's Progress, in the fullest sense of the word.

Landing on the Field of Battle.

The following day I landed at Puerto Montt. The navigation between the numerous islands of Chiloe is somewhat dangerous; but what a sight for the traveler! It is the archipelego of the Pacific. The pleasure of this trip surpasses all description, and I could only say: "Come and see." The inhabitants of these islands are poor but good-natured half-breeds, and excellent farm hands. The south and north of Chili are supplied with laborers from these islands. The Romish priests have done more for these people than perhaps for any other on the *terra firma* of Chili and the entire West Coast. Most of these people can read and write. But of course they are terribly superstitious, and never read any other books except such as are given them by the priest, and only those of lowest order.

Leaving the steamer I went at once to the hotel, and gave myself wholly up to prayer. How I longed for a few days of seclusion after so long a sea-voyage! I wanted to be alone with God,—my soul was craving for God, to see Him alone, when no one was near to disturb or observe. I felt so peaceful, and I could commit myself and all into His hands, and talk with Him who had thus guided me. In my room I stood alone, but I knew God was with me. There was no invitation to a revival, with such an outlook as I had been accustomed to at home, — not just in the same way; but was it not the same Jesus, the same blessed promise beneath me? Was the promise not the same to me to-day as ever, that "every place where my foot shall tread upon, had been given unto me," and that "As I was with Moses, so shall I be with thee" (Joshua i.)? Ah, yes! the text was applied, and, bless the Lord! my soul looked up to the Mighty to Save, and for that cause I bowed my knees there and then, and there the Lord talked with me.

My First German Sermon.

In a few hours the whole village knew that I had arrived, and that I was a preacher, and very soon some one knocked at my door, and a kind-hearted, good-natured German stepped in and invited me to preach in the school-house "to-morrow," (this being Saturday). The good man told me that the pastor, Mr. S., had gone to the lake, and would stay there a few weeks, as he did four times every year, during which time he baptized and confirmed the children, and preached on the Sabbath. I consented at once that I would preach. Then I tried to find out all about the work in the town, and in the province; and by the time the man got through, I could look upon myself as a kind of intruder, although I could plainly see that the Lutheran brother could never do all the work that was to be done in the province of Llanquihue, nor that any two men could do justice to the demands of the field; but I well understood the German clergy, and I betook myself to earnest prayer and meditation, that I might have wisdom to act wisely in the matter; and, after prayer, I concluded to start out on Monday and meet Mr. S. at the Lake, where he now was, preaching. This was to be the first step.

It being somewhat late, I dismissed my German landsman, and prepared for bed. I had not talked so much German for six years as I had been compelled to this evening, and I found that it was hard for me. "How peculiar," I thought: "a full-blooded Dutchman, and almost forgotten his mother tongue!" I wondered how it would be in the morning, to preach to the people. I had never preached in the German language — had never in my life handled a German Bible, nor a theological book in that language. My head began to turn on its axis, and I gave up thought, and fell sweetly asleep in Jesus' arms of love.

The morning came, and with it the certainty that I had to face a German congregation, for the first time since I was in the service of my Master. I felt the perspiration starting through the pores of the skin about the forehead. It was different from that feeling which I often experienced before preaching to a congregation, and especially when persons are present who, I think, are so much better than myself, or know how to preach better than myself, or some such awkward feeling.

This was quite a new experience. But I was still more confounded when I took up my German Bible and tried to think "in German," and at last, walking up and down in my room, tried to talk and get at it in that way; but the best I could do was simply to break out in laughing aloud at myself, and throwing myself across the bed and laughing until I could laugh no more. But I made another manly effort: it was simply ridiculous. The hour for preaching drew near, and I grew strangely serious. I then began to cry and weep and pray, and then it came to me that I had been real foolish, and it seemed to whisper, "What are you fretting about?" That put me to shame, and I felt that I blushed. I then took my English Bible, selected my text, "Naaman the Syrian," laid it down, and taking my German Bible, started for the school-house, where the people were already waiting, and had thronged the place. I went, simply trusting that God would fill my mouth, and placing myself, limber-like, in His hands, I now had rest; and with a peaceful mind and leaning pretty hard on the Master, I read my lesson and pronounced my text, and then came the preaching.

I think I shall never forget that hour. It seemed that I must have always been preaching in German. I was blessed, and evidently the people were blessed; but one came to me and said: "Mr. K., you several times used entire English words, which I could not make out." All right! Praise the Lord! The ice was broken, and after all there was no giant to scare me.

The Colony on Lake Llanquihue.

The following morning a German came and offered me a horse to ride to the Lake, and while preparing for this, my first journey in Chili on *terra firma*, a letter from the pastor was handed to me, in which he invited me to meet him at a certain station at the Lake, from whence we would proceed to Osorno, to meet the pastor stationed there, and have a conference together, and see what arrangements could be made between us. Now, this looked encouraging, and sounded like business. So after another precious talk with Jesus, I started, and being mounted on a spirited little Indian pony, and accompanied by a German guide, we soon reached the Lake. On the way out I stopped at nearly every house, greeting the people, reading Scripture, and praying before leaving the house. These poor people had never seen any such proceedings, and I saw they had been entirely neglected. Many a warm grasp of the hand I felt, and many a tear glistening in the eyes of the older members of the different households. From this one visit new life and new hopes seemed to have been revived, and this journey was a blessed one to me and to all. Yet I felt the contest for the possession of that field would be hard, but God could give us the victory.

From this out our road became very rough — narrow paths, up and down hill, through numberless rivers and little streams, mud-holes, and closely-edging steep precipices. Every half hour we found a colonist, either working near his house, or, with his peones, cutting down the dense forests, and burning the dried branches and trunks of trees, getting the soil ready for the reception of wheat. I saw splendid cattle and sheep and horses in abundance, and all the colonists, without any exception, seemed to do well.

How My Landsmen Live.

The people were very kind and friendly. In every place they insisted that I should dismount, and either drink milk or wheat coffee, and eat black bread and German sausage. It seemed hard to refuse, and yet I could not make them believe that I was full " to split," but what should I do, even though I had to wait in one house and see how the good lady of the house emptied a bowl of dirty soap-water, and filling it with good beef soup, placed it before me, and delivered her lecture on the quality of the soup in most eloquent style? I had better keep the secret to myself. I was struck with the untidiness of most of those farmers about the Lake; things looked wild in many a household, and they seemed to take no pleasure in cleanliness and reasonable comfort. They might all have enjoyed both. However, they were glad when I read from the Bible to them, and prayed with them. I had the pleasure of meeting an Englishman, who owned a farm here. He had come over from Australia with a wife and five children, and bought this farm, and was doing very well. His wife I found to be a thorough Christian woman, but very sick. She had been confined to her bed for several years, yet she rejoiced in the Lord. She also tried to train her children in that way. The boys were grown, but were not Christians; the girls were like their mother.

After a day's ride on horseback, we had reached, late in the evening, a whiskey distillery, and my guide told me that here we must stay over night, and take up the road on to-morrow, and that we would meet the pastor, Mr. S., by to-morrow noon. I did not like the idea of lodging at this distillery very much. The room was filled with colonists, and a great deal of beer and whiskey was drank, and of course I was invited on every hand to partake of the cup. I pitied these poor people, when I noticed the looks of astonishment at my stout refusal, and on cigars being offered I did the same. The people could not understand this at all. When I gave them my reasons for not drinking beer and not smoking cigars, they felt inclined to respect me for my total abstinence; but thought it was a great pity, as their pastor knew how to enjoy both these things, they said. When, after a while, I had to refuse to play cards, they thought me to be "holy" — an awful thing among them. On the whole, they had never seen such a person before, especially a clergyman, who would not drink, nor smoke, nor play cards. I noticed the dear people were stumbling over it; and thinking it was time to explain somewhat of the reason of the hope that was in me, I began to tell them something about the eleventh commandment. That did its work, and they seemed to see the expediency of my mode of life from that standpoint, better than if I had brought up all the arguments in the world to prove my point. And when I added the testimony as to what Jesus did for me, they sat in silence, with open ears and eyes, and in the eyes of some of the older members of the company one could see the tears. These arose by and by, shook my hand, and said: " This did me good," and silently separated from the company, and went their way home. I was much pleased with this little interview with some of the people, who, I hoped, would be my hearers in the near future.

Early the next morning my guide and I were on our way to Punto de los Chamchos, — called so from the formation of a neck of land running out into the lake, resembling a "pig's head," and there, at a farmer's house, Mr. S. was waiting for me. It did not take us as long as I had thought. The horses were rested, and the road considerably better, so we reached our destination about 10.30 A. M.

The farmer, a sturdy, friendly-looking German, met me at the door, and was evidently glad to see me; next came out wife, daughter, and son,—all seemed to be glad to welcome me to their home; last of all came my brother pastor. The reception was cold and entirely formal. However, I was not disappointed. I understood a young man had come over from the distillery, early this morning, a few hours before me, and had announced my coming; also giving a report of what he had seen and heard there.

The New Idea,—"A Holy Man."

The reverend gentleman had made up his mind to the fact that I must be a "holy man," and received me accordingly. Very little was said during the day, my friend trying very hard to impress me with the fact that he was "lording it" over the people, and he was a great deal more learned than they were; which I, however, never disputed for a moment; and also with the certainty that he could smoke more cigars and drink more beer than I could. The evening in the room was spent in relating something about my late travels, and gathering information respecting this country, and the colony in particular. The smoke from the Dutch pipes of my two friends — the farmer and the parson —

threatened to suffocate me; but I stood it in good grace, and had no complaints to make. But when every bit of pure air had been most effectually excluded from the low room, the good parson offered me a Havana, which was promptly refused, and I turned to wipe my "weeping eyes." There was not much emotion, but the smoke bit my eyes terribly. I noticed soon that this cigar had been simply offered to test the truthfulness of this morning's messenger. I had, up to the time, carefully avoided any signs of disapproval as to the proceedings of the evening, and the German parson could not hold in any longer — he must satisfy his curiosity, and see for himself whether the report concerning me was true or not. I was then called upon to give a reason for my moderation, and in the most charitable way I told these two men the story of love, — of course, understanding that I dealt with two blind men, and sick at that, I dealt cautiously, and in the most loving way, — about as the doctor would make castor oil go down easy, — only I could not help the effect.

First Signs of Opposition.

I felt exceedingly sorry when I saw I had made myself obnoxious to my friend, the parson. But I believe he felt more hurt that I knew my sins forgiven, than at anything else. He knew I would not join in his way of "passing away time,"— a fashionable term used by some of the clergy and laity now-a-days, — a sort of a "sheepskin" suit, of course it is calculated to deceive: it is n't sheepskin after all, it's only a whitewash, and used to paint over "sore spots," and makes those using the stuff only look worse. Poor deluded creatures! God have mercy on poor sinners, and the blind leading the blind.

The following morning my guide returned to his home, and mounting fresh horses, Mr. S. and myself left our hospitable friends and journeyed towards Osorno. We could not reach it in one day, so we stopped over night at an inn, on the extreme northern shore of the lake. Several children were baptized there, and I made the acquaintance of nearly all the farmers in that neighborhood, for the Germans are very fond of spending their evenings at the inn, and do n't mind walking or riding for hours to reach it; but more especially when the parson is announced to be there, as he was very fond of talking about cattle, beer, tobacco, and family affairs. The only good that I could see was done in those gatherings, was that they did their quarrelling and fighting at the inn, instead of aggravating their poor, hard-worked wives and children at home.

Their Forlorn Condition.

But those poor never-dying souls were left uncared for. Oh, how my heart yearned after them! but I had seen enough to show me that the field would be a difficult one; but, also, that preaching Christ crucified would finally reach the people. They seemed to be totally ignorant of the fact that Jesus Christ came into the world to actually save from sin, and that it was obligatory to search the Scriptures to derive from them saving knowledge. I found these poor people had never been disturbed, and on that ground I had some hope. Give them a fair chance, and they will seek the Saviour of the world. I felt from that hour that God had laid these precious souls upon my heart, and in His name I would go and preach the word of life. Many of the children of these colonists I found, who had grown up without religious training, and in, oh, how many cases! had not even learned to read or write; and some of such had only just married, and in either case, as to the man or the woman, I found this to be a sad fact. If the condition of these was bad, what would in turn become of their children? I did not wonder when the pastor himself informed me, as we rode on the next morning, that it was quite common among the people at the Lake, that sons and daughters would abuse and maltreat their old parents, having no respect for them. But alas! he himself had never become acquainted with Jesus, and how could he lead this people?

I talked much with God that day, as we went on our way to Osorno, and entertained but little hope that the man stationed there would be a different man, but felt I might be opposed by them, and the way should be closed against me to work at the Lake. My love for that people had already been kindled, and I was burning to bring to them the word of Christ, and through it make them acquainted with a purer and truly noble life, and with a conscious indwelling holiness.

After a ride of six hours, partly through dense forests, which I could not help but compare with the finest tropical forests, and in parts with an Indian jungle, we reached Osorno, a place where about 1500 Germans live. It had the appearance of thrift, and I understood the extensive cattle raising in these parts, and the large tanneries, gave the place a name in the southern parts of Chili. However, the number of breweries and whiskey distilleries astonished me. The Germans here have a large school and a neat little chapel. I was soon introduced to the Rev. Mr. R., the preacher in charge, and also director of the school. I found him a very pleasant man, who received me warmly, and his kindness was genuine. I felt much encouraged, and hoped that matters would be satisfactorily arranged. We chatted on general subjects a few hours, and then we separated for the evening, in order to rest and refresh ourselves with sleep, and to meet in the morning of the following day for conference. There was no family altar in the house, and we left for our rooms without praying together. This did not impress me favorably; and being alone, I poured out my heavy but trustful heart to my God. I thought of Bro. Hoffmann, whom I had left at Valdivia, and almost envied him for his position; and I remembered the words of an old man whom I met on his farm, at the Lake, who said, taking hold of my hand, and with tears in his eyes: " I wish you had come to us twenty years ago, before any other man began to preach here." Perhaps he was right. I truly believe that Christless ministers of the Gospel, who are not witnesses, do incalculable harm, both at home, and more especially, in mission fields. " I have called thee to be a minister and a witness." I like that word which came directly down from heaven. God does not want any ministers unless they are witnesses to the cleansing and purifying power of the blood of Jesus, for how can I lead souls nearer to God than I am myself? God make me to be a swift witness while I remain on earth, or else blot me out of the book of the ministry!

A Conference.

Much refreshed after so much riding on horseback, I arose in the morning, and after my morning Scripture lesson and a sweet talk with Jesus, I met the two Lutheran pastors in the study. I at once set to work and told them what I had come for, and that I thought Bro. S. had a great deal of work on hand, and if agreeable,

I should, with the help of God, go to work among the people at the Lake colony, as I thought the pastoral hurried visits of four times in the year could never do justice to the wants of the people. I freely spoke out my impressions which I had received during my trip and by conversing with the people, with due respect, giving credit to the work that had been attempted by Mr. S. Bro. R. seconded all that I had to say. He said he knew the people, and had often thought they should be better cared for; but that it was impossible for either one of them to do them justice, the distance being so great, and the colonists much scattered. He thought that a preacher should be stationed at the Lake, and furthermore he felt to congratulate Mr. S. upon my arrival, as he thought, just in time, and that my coming was of God. What Mr. R. said was thoroughly evangelical, and I liked the man very much, as I thought he had at least good feeling towards the people, and that he was more liberal than his colleague, who had all this time said nothing. When his turn came he raised many objections. He thought that I was too strict, and that his people at the Lake would never agree with me. In fact, he feared everything for me that he could think of. Yes, perhaps I thought he had good reason to fear, and I felt for him. It took a great deal of persuasion on the part of my evangelical friend, and at last he yielded, but reluctantly. I did not exactly like it much, to see that his heart was not in it; but I hoped the man might be brought to see for himself. My position was, however, at best, not one that I much desired; but what could I do? The Lord had some work for me to do here, and He would stand by me; so everything was committed to God, and I was determined to go on.

The remainder of the day I spent in visiting some of the families in the town, and had precious experiences. In one house a young lady was brought under conviction for sin, and I believed the Lord would convert her.

CHAPTER VI.

THE COMMENCEMENT OF WORK IN THE COLONIES.

I STAYED only a few days in the place, and then hurried back to the Lake, to take up my work at once. I visited now from house to house, reading Scripture and praying with the people. The results in many instances were most gratifying, and I saw that the Lord did a wonderful work of conviction for sin. Although they seemed to be so ignorant of Biblical truth, yet they understood the testimony concerning an "every-day Christ; and illustrating Scripture by personal experience, brought on the deep conviction for sin, and a burning desire to receive the same blessing of pardon followed. In every home I received a most hearty welcome — plenty to eat and a good feather-bed, as well as guides and fast horses, without paying for them. The two ministers in Osorno had told me that my support would be rather a slim affair, as the people at the Lake had pledged themselves for three years to raise a certain sum every year to help support the work at Puerto Montt, of which place Mr. S. was the pastor, and without which support the mission at Puerto Montt could not get along. Mr. S., in yielding up the field to me, would not let that part of the arrangement with the people slip, and thought that he would still now and then visit the people and baptize their children, and that if I could get a support among them outside of that, I should go on. Of course I agreed to that, and hoped that the Lord would open my way, and I would trust Him for my daily bread and clothing.

There were no less than from five to six whiskey distilleries around the Lake, and the owners of these mills were getting alarmed, and tried to hinder the work, and they found a man — the pastor of Puerto Montt — who now began to work against me with every possible means at his command. He knew I was a Methodist. Papers from Germany, such as were always full of slurs against that denomination, were imported and scattered among the people, and especially those who had a name among the colonists. I soon had those who held the money, and were able to buy up the wheat and the cattle, all against me, and there were hot fights every day. In the midst of all these oppositions, however, the Lord converted souls. Some found peace, and it stirred the neighborhood tremendously, and some of the people became almost infuriated against the work, being constantly fed with bad reports concerning the Methodists. But just then one of the whiskey distillers seemed to be friendly disposed, and offered me the free use of a house that was unoccupied at the time. I accepted the offer, and took good courage, working hard every day, constantly visiting from house to house, and praying and preaching whenever an opportunity offered itself. The people were wonderfully wrought upon, and some were mad.

After thus laboring for a few months, I visited Osorno, and had an interview with the pastor. He had heard all about the mad persecutions instigated by Mr. S., and had already written to him; but thought it would help nothing. Mr. S. had taken his stand against me, and now he would not yield in any point. Mr. S. had told him that the people turned crazy, and that the peace of the colony was much disturbed. I did not doubt it a moment. The devil had held sway at the Lake these many years, and now began to kick, — the only hopeful sign for their souls, and, thanks be to God, some few had found the Saviour.

The First Convert.

I did some visiting in the town before I left, and found the young German lady mentioned before, trusting in the Saviour. Soon after I had left Osorno, after my first visit, she had found peace. *It was the first convert in my work in South America.* Praise the Lord! She seemed wonderfully gifted in prayer, and manifested a child-like faith in the new-found Saviour. On my way back to the Lake, I made an arrangement with some of the people, who could not send their children to school because of the distance they had to go, that I would start a school at my house for boys and girls, and make arrangements to board and lodge them, provided that the parents furnish the bedding and a certain amount of flour or wheat and potatoes, and such vegetables as would be necessary and convenient, to be sent each month in a boat across the Lake, to where I lived. They liked the idea, and I gave them a fixed time to think over it, and send me the names of the children, and the day when they should be sent. On my arrival home, I found a letter, which I recognized to be one from Bro. Hoffman; but to my great surprise, read that he had just arrived at Puerto Montt, and that he had been compelled to leave Valdivia. My first object was to hurry on to Puerto Montt, and see what all this meant, for I hardly knew where to put Bro. H., when I knew he could not be supported here.

I met him, full of faith and the Holy Ghost, yet sorrowful that Valdivia had to be given up. He had suffered terribly there. He and dear Sister H. had been shamefully slandered, and in every conceivable way persecuted, until at last, although reluctantly, the place was given up.

Bro. H. had called a meeting at the school-house, in order to talk to the people and make some arrangement for his remaining in the city. Many came, exclusively men, bringing with them their long German pipes, and sufficient tobacco and cigars to fill, in a short time, the room with smoke, to suffocation, and keeping up loud talking and such a noise that Bro. H. never had a chance to speak; and although he asked those present to lend him an ear, they did not regard him. In fact, the men, to all intent, purposed to drive out Bro. Hoffman. Nothing could be accomplished, and Bro. H. left the room with a heavy heart; however, not intending to give up the struggle so soon, they found a friendly family with whom they lived a short time, and the enemies of the Cross not being satisfied with their work of persecuting Bro. H., turned upon all those who came in friendly contact with him, and their anger was kindled against those who had taken Bro. H. and wife to their house. Most shameful reports were spread concerning them, and at last they were compelled to ask Bro. Hoffman to leave the house. Bro. H. did all he could to remain and get a footing, but it seemed the Lord permitted these things. The people of Valdivia had an offer of salvation, and this time rejected it.

Bro. H., without first writing to me about his intentions of coming to Puerto Montt, started at once, and thus we met again. On the south side of the Lake, the Lord had raised us up a friend, who offered to Bro. Hoffman a small house which was not in use at the time, and told him to live there as long as he liked, and he would not charge him anything for rent. So it was decided that Bro. H. should move to the Lake, and do whatever the Lord might have for him to do, — truly the harvest was ripe and the laborers but few. I returned to my post as soon as I had seen Bro. H. and wife sheltered, and I found that about six children had applied for admission to the school. It was a beginning, and I hoped the dear children would become true Christians, and I would have the means of a subsistence, and the Gospel take healthy root in the soil, and spread more and more in the neighborhood; and the same time thought Bro. H. would do the same.

Taken Prisoner.

Before opening my school, I again started for Osorno, but this time on a more important errand, and a little different from the first. I had felt for some little time previous that some time or other I would have to take an important step toward settling down in life, and form a household of my own. After much prayer on the subject, I decided to take the step, and humbly asked God to bless me in the selection of my future partner in life. The one whom the Lord had given me as the first-fruit of my labors in Chili, I had selected, and I felt I loved her so dearly that I could ask her to become my wife. I cannot tell how I felt when journeying to the place, which contained what, next to God, and the souls of the lost, I loved most on earth; but I do know what I felt when, taking her hand, I asked her to become my wife, and when she said "I will." But I propose to keep it all to myself, what I then felt.

In the evening I received an invitation from father and mother, and soon we all met in the happy family circle. Both parents blessed us, and then we knelt in prayer to receive the Heavenly Father's blessing, which was richly bestowed upon us all. The aged mother then said: "I have eight sons, but this is the only daughter; we love each other much; but take her. You are a man of God, and I need say no more. I shall rest." In two weeks after this event, we were united in holy matrimony, Bro. Hoffman officiating. It was a solemn hour, and God was with us.

A MISSIONARY'S PLEASANT TRIP TO A WEDDING.

I had gone to the north side of the Lake to meet Bro. Hoffman with his wife, and had hired horses to take them to Osorno. Bro. H. and his good wife were not accustomed to ride much on horseback, and Bro. Hoffman behaved rather awkwardly in the saddle. I called his attention to the stirrup and the reins, and he jokingly remarked that I had better take care of myself; and of course, between us the trip was much enjoyed, although I disturbed Bro. Hoffman's mind considerably, and complimented him on his excellent (?) horsemanship;

but this all would have been endurable if the poor animal had not stumbled "just a little," just then, and thrown poor Henry over its head, with force enough to send him about fifteen yards ahead, and completely rolled up and hid away in his large *ponsho* — a square woollen blanket with an opening in the centre to admit the head — thus serving for a mantle, and a good protection against dust or rain, — a garment universally worn in South America. While the good brother extricated himself from his *ponsho*, I started in another direction to pick up his fine tall hat, and yonder the cover of the hat-box, and somewhere else the lower half of the box. After joining things a bit, and as soon as we could quit laughing and scramble into our saddles, we started again on our way, rejoicing that no bones had been broken, only the brass handle to the hat-box missing. All that Bro. H. said was, that he didn't know how in the world this could have happened, — in fact, he didn't know how he got off the horse. I thought I had better not explain, and he did not show any resistance. We agreed to say nothing more about it, and the horse did not stumble any more.

We soon reached an inn, and we were glad to rest for a short time, and refresh ourselves with some good milk, bread, and cheese.

Half an hour later we had to pass a very bad place on the road — a great mud-hole; but being well acquainted in these parts, I took the lead and bade my brother and sister follow in the same track. I got across all right, and dismounting, I turned and gave directions to the two. Sister Katie followed, but she was very timid, and I called to her to take firm hold on the saddle with one hand, and with the other the horse's mane. The horse was a very gentle little animal, and stepped very carefully, drawing out of the mud one leg after another, which, however, caused him to lean over a little on one side as he walked, and every time Sister Katie feared lest she should fall over into the mud. The animal was just placing the right foot on *terra firma*, when I heard a scream. Sister Katie let go her hold and fell right over, backwards, into the mud, head first, of course, and almost disappeared beneath the troubled waves, — well, not waves either, the mud was a little too stiff for that, and it would seem too poetic. Really, it was not reminding of anything very poetic, when I jumped right after her, while Bro. H. remained on his horse like one " struck with an idea," and began fishing. Soon our tired horses were standing on firm ground, and we did not look pretty, — no, decidedly not; but we were alive, and while helping each other to scrape the mud off, we did good work biting our lips to keep from shouting outright, until we just concluded it was no use, and let come what would. Well, we pitied poor Sister Hoffman, and I did my best to comfort her, and tried to assure her in every way of my sympathy, although I did not succeed as well as I wished for. Then we tried to make our horses respectable looking, but that was rather hard work, and we gave it up. We men divested ourselves now of our *ponshos*, and wrapping them about our sister as well as I could, we then rode on, trying to reach Osorno as late as possible, and showing no desire for further investigation of the condition of things along the road; although a number of opportunities were offered. Sister Katie hoped she would soon learn to ride, and the comfort of such a thought seemed to do her good.

After spending a week at the house of my father-in-law, I departed with my wife to the Lake, put our house in order, and now received our pupils. When school was opened I had ten children — the youngest being twelve years old, and the oldest a girl of twenty-two -- a native, — all of whom could not read or write. There was work to be done, indeed. There were at least fifty more of the same age, and not better taught. My good wife and I loved our children, and they learned well, but we had as yet not received anything to live upon; the children had brought the bedding, but nothing had come to eat, and for a little time we had nothing except what we received in direct answer to prayer. One day when we had nothing in the house, and had nothing to give to the children, and the boats not being able to come across the Lake, as was expected, on account of stormy weather, we bowed to God in prayer, as we had done so often before, and while praying we heard a knock at the door, and opening the door we saw a good Bro. K., who had come a distance of two hours on horseback, and as he unpacked from his saddle-bags a good lot of provisions — a large bladder of butter, a ham, some smoked sausages, and two large loaves of bread, and some fruit — he told us that in the morning he felt troubled in his heart concerning us, and following the impression he thus received, concluded that he would take with him these things and see us. When we told him that we had expected something like it, he was much overjoyed, and was glad that he had come.

Support came in very sparingly for Bro. Hoffman, and also for us; but we never lacked anything. Bro. H. had a similar experience, and he also received his bread in direct answer to prayer. One day we received quite a boat-load of provisions from the parents of the children we had with us, and it was sufficient for a month; but no money came in from our people here to buy us the necessary clothing. But we looked again to God, and in a few days we received $200 from some friends at Valparaiso — half for Bro. H.

The Conversion of Ten Children.

The work of salvation was going on gloriously among our children, and every one of them professed conversion by this time, and all prayed as the Spirit gave them utterance, around the family altar. My wife had received a piano from her father, and she taught the children to sing the sweet songs of Zion, and when the people gathered on the Sabbath for public worship, they were much blessed in hearing these new hymns (I had translated some from the Moody and Sankey hymns). We had received some German hymn-books, which Bro. Hoffmann had brought with him from the States. It looked now, as far as the school was concerned, as though we should succeed. The children could give a reason for the hope that was within them, and they boldly confessed the Saviour.

But a storm was brewing. The persecutions from the outside were intensifying, and at last the time came when certain parties had so far succeeded as to cause some of my patrons to take their children from the school. The poor children would cry, and lament, and they would not quit singing their beautiful hymns, nor would they neglect their prayers; and a cry arose that the children were being led astray, and away from the old religion of the church. Times of great trial came upon us, and for a time the sky seemed very dark; but in these seasons of affliction the Saviour never deserted us; we felt His presence more than ever; and then, when the time came that we felt the work had better cease, we did not understand it, but we would follow Jesus and He should lead us. We had at last only three children, and oh, how hard it seemed to part from them! We felt as though they were our own; but they said: "We will not forget or deny Jesus, and we'll tell our parents about Jesus when we get home." So we sent them away to their homes, while my wife, with myself, prepared to visit Bro. Hoffman, in order that we might take counsel as to what was best to do. It was clear to my mind that one of us would have to leave the field. Bro. H. had passed through similar experiences; but it was decided, he having no relatives in this country, that he should remain at the post, while I concluded to go to Osorno and remain at my father-in-law's, and await answer from Valparaiso as to an opening there for a lasting work in which to finally establish ourselves and do work for God, if the people wanted us.

Bro. Hoffman and I made another visiting tour around the Lake, and we met with blessed success.

A Roman Catholic Family Converted to God.

Visiting a Roman Catholic family where the Lord had, through Bro. H., converted the daughter, we found the mother, father, and a son, under conviction for sin.

They invited us to stay over night. We accepted the invitation, and God wonderfully blessed our visit to that house. While kneeling in prayer, the mother could not hold back any longer, and after her daughter had prayed for her dear father and brother and mother, she burst out in tears, and making her humble confession to God, accepted the Saviour to be her Saviour from sin. Bro. Hoffman, kneeling close to the son, — eighteen years old — asked him to come in prayer to God. His father heard it and said: "Oh, he is like his father! he can't pray or say a word before strangers"; but just then the son opened his mouth and poured forth his soul in such earnest prayer for the pardon of his sins, that we all wept with him; and also, in the end, before rising with him, we could rejoice with him, for he found his Saviour. The boy's father was all broken up when he saw what was done, and he also stammered his plea for pardon. Somehow we had moved close up to each other on our knees, and there was a scene which angels love to behold. A whole family born again! Glory to God! There was great joy in that house. Truly God had done great things here.

After much prayer, we concluded to visit the pastor at Puerto Montt, and ask him to cease his persecutions, and to relieve the people of their contract with him, so that Bro. H. could stay among the people and receive some support. We accordingly set out on our errand, and had a meeting with Mr. S. He felt very uneasy when he was confronted by us; however, he tried to deny the charges brought against him; but it was a vain attempt. But we did not desire to trouble him on that line; but rather come to some arrangement concerning Bro. H. Mr. S. would not yield a point, and thought that we better both go, as this was his field of labor. He was right in one sense, and we had a weak point there, certainly; but to prove to him that he could not do the work, and that two or three more men could be very useful in that field, we could not; at any rate, to say the least, he felt convinced that we were not those two men who ought to do that work, or help him to do it.

I then spoke to him about the result of our work, and asked him to compare it with the former work, or the condition of those professing conversion previous to our coming. There we touched a sore spot, and the poor man grew quite excited. He thought we were wolves in sheep's clothing, and deceiving the people, and only working to put him out of the way. Things looked very dark indeed, and we utterly failed to come to any terms with him. We took our departure, and Bro. Hoffman told him that he should remain, although I would soon leave.

Bro. Taylor had never been to this place when he visited the West Coast of South America two years ago.

He only heard from the colporteur of the Bible Society at Valparaiso; who, being a German, had ten years ago visited these colonies, in the interest of his Society, and there met with success, both in preaching and the selling of good books, and reported to William Taylor as he had found things then. Otherwise, these great troubles might have been avoided.

However, many precious souls have found the Saviour, and I feel that for the experience I have had here, I am greatly strengthened, and hope to be more fit for future work in winning souls for the kingdom of God, than heretofore. I feel that I have to learn so much, and I pray to my God that all may redound to His glory, what here I was permitted to endure and undergo. Thanks be to God, who keepeth my soul in perfect peace and joy in the Holy Ghost. Amen.

A Trying Change.

Thus I left Bro. Hoffman in this field, not with brightest prospects of reconciling existing difficulties with his earnest and faithful labors; but with a firm hope that something would give way, and peace be established, and the work of God go on unhindered. Before leaving his home, however, I had the satisfaction of hearing the testimonies of the old man and his wife, who had permitted Bro. H. to occupy their house. They both had found the Saviour, and were conscious of a perfect salvation from sin. Thus God was pleased to honor his servant along life's roughest road. Glory be to God in the highest!

Just then came a gift of $40 to each of us from Valparaiso. The Lord knew what we stood in need of, and supplied us accordingly. Bro. Hoffman's experience on the faith line was something wonderful, and we were a great comfort to each other while being privileged to spend a few days together. God had led us truly wonderfully, in these days of trouble and fiery persecutions; but we had come out the brighter in experience and faith toward God.

We separated. It seemed so hard. We wept on each other's necks. We had passed through deep waters in a comparatively short space of time. For a moment the past swept by once more, and in it all we could but see that the Lord had been with us, and that nothing was to be regretted. Another hearty shake of the hand — a holy kiss and embrace — and our horses gallopped rapidly across the pampas, over into the road leading to our home, which was soon to be vacated again. I loved the spot where our home stood — about two-hundred feet above the level of the Lake at our feet, surrounded by beautiful trees of the forest, open towards the water; and away across the beautiful Lake, directly opposite our house, arose the volcano — Osorno — 2500 metres above the waters of the Lake, covered with everlasting snow. I loved to watch the sunset right back of our house, casting its golden hues against the snow-fields of the volcano, transforming it into a mighty mass of glowing lava; or the moon decking it with silvery carpet. Nature seems so lovely here; but then the picture of sin rises to the front, with all its horrors, and dripping with the tears of those under the power of the prince of darkness. But in nature we had a Paradise. It is the spot that our feet did cover. There, with God, what could make its possession bitter? And then we are reminded of God's word in Joshua i. 2, and that is the word, and it is our spiritual Paradise, heaven in the soul, — God — Jesus — all. Amen.

My last sermon was to be preached at the farm-house of one of the colonists, about a mile off. It was large, and would accommodate more people than our own. The following Sabbath we were to meet them, probably for the last time on earth.

A Sure Way to get Bad Roads Repaired.

The next day the justice of the peace came to me and said: "You are going to preach next Sunday at the house of Mr. S.?" — "Yes, I shall preach there." — "Well, you had better get him to repair the road leading past his farm, and you'll do a better thing than to be preaching nonsense to the people. I have been to Mr. S. very often about that road, but he refuses to obey. That's the sort of people that want you to preach to them."

This man was an unbeliever, and had often before laughed at the children who visited my school, and often asked them questions; but the children would give such answers that he was put to shame, and gave up troubling them any more. Now he came to me and thought to make light of the power of the Gospel to make men new creatures. I told him, since he had given Mr. S. up, the Lord would take him in hand, and the road would not only be fixed, but Mr. S. would be a happy man and a good neighbor. The infidel sneered at me, and said he would never see it done.

I was much troubled concerning S. He had been to my meetings several times, and I knew him to be anything but a good neighbor, and he was very obstinate man; and I also was well acquainted with that bad road, for many times I feared that my horse would not be able to carry me over it. I prayed that day much for poor Mr. S., and in the afternoon my mind was made up to ride over and see him. However, I had no message to give him concerning the repairing of the road, but I did feel burdened about his soul; and when I took him by the hand, and was alone with him, I told him that I had been much exercised about his soul all day, and that I came to tell him to give his heart to Jesus. I reminded him how that he had heard the word of God so often, and that now he had given his house for the last service to be held in this colony, and that I thought something was going on in his heart. I had noticed that while I was speaking to him, his head dropped; and when he looked at me again, when I had finished, his eyes were filled with tears, and he told me that he had been troubled all day, too, and that we might as well have a word of prayer now, and settle the question with the Lord. So we knelt down and prayed. First I prayed, and then he prayed for himself. The prayer was answered immediately, and he found peace and confessed it joyfully. My message was delivered, and the Lord had taken care of the results, and we now parted, hoping to meet day after to-morrow, on the Sabbath.

Sunday morning we rode over to what was now *Bro. S.* But what did we find before we reached the house? Why, we hardly believed our eyes, — we scarcely recognized the spot where once was the bad road. Trees and bushes had been cut down, a narrow bridge had been constructed to allow the water to run off freely, and great labor had evidently been spent here only recently, to put the road into proper shape. I guessed it all, and praised the Lord for what He had done. Bro. S. met us on the road, and reaching out both hands, bade us a hearty good morning, and then said: "Well, Bro. K., after you had left my house on Friday, I thought it was high time to fix that road, and that you should travel over that road to my house on Sunday dry shod, and I experienced great pleasure in repairing it; but, thanks be to God! I really did it it to glorify God, for the people have been after me for some time about that road." When people get converted to God, they always will do right. That is just what religion will do for man. It will clean up filthy houses when the hearts are emptied of filthy sin. It will repair bad roads, if once the highway for the King has been cast up in the soul. Thanks be to God for a heartfelt religion! Amen. Praise the Lord!

We had a glorious Gospel feast that day, and the wife of Bro. S. was converted to God, and some others seemed to be convicted of sin. One old man said: "Oh, it is so hard to take hold of God after serving the devil so many years! I have the Bible at my house, and am reading in it sometimes to appease my troubled conscience; but I never was in real earnest, and the truth was not disclosed to me, and I know I am as far away from God as ever." Poor man! He wept, but could not lay hold upon Christ. I left him in that condition; but trust he will yet find pardon. How dangerous it is to wait and carelessly live in sin! The Lord will not be mocked; what a man soweth, that shall he also reap. Scripture is terribly true, and it says (Prov. v. 21), "His own iniquities shall take the wicked, and he shall be holden with the cords of his sin." How hard it seems to break loose when we find how the cords of our sins bind us down! Practice and habit — who shall deliver us from the body of this death? Thanks be to God, through Jesus our Lord, and only through Him, we can be delivered. Without deliverance through Jesus we are ever wretched. The Lord save the people.

CHAPTER VII.

A CHANGE TO THE CITY.

OUR work was done in these parts, and precious seed had been sown to the last. What will the harvest be? Thanks be to God, we knew the work of God did not end with our going. The promise that the word should accomplish that whereunto it had been sent, was just as good now as ever it was before. God is still the husbandman, and He who causes the birds of the air and the winds to carry the little grains of seed to the bare and rocky mountains, where in some way they germinate, strike root, and grow up to praise the Maker, will not suffer that one of His blessed words, bearing the germ of eternal life, should be lost. As storms, and rains, and cold, and heat, only seem to contribute to preserve the former until it has accomplished its design, so in the latter case, no odds, no human power nor devilish ragings, shall prevail against it. The storms of ages shall fan the spark to blazing fire. There I rest it with God. Praise His name!

We bade adieu to our cottage on the hill — we waved our hand across the beautiful Lake, and the volcano had hid its form behind a pure white cloud. Our hearts were sorely tried; but thus our God permitted it all. One last look as we reached the northern extremes of the Lake, and then our road turned sharp to the west. In ten hours we reached Osorno.

A Wonderful Deliverance on Horseback.

Ten hours on horseback; but both my dear wife and I were tolerable riders, and we felt not over-tired, when, late that day — it was 9.30 p. m. — we reached the parental homestead. However, before reaching the city, it being very dark, in crossing a bridge we did not observe the defective condition of the same, and I had just passed across, when behind me I heard the bridge, with a loud crash, break down, beneath the weight of the horse and its precious burden. But just as I alighted from my horse to run to assist my poor wife, whom I supposed to be, at least, severely hurt, the horse and rider stood beside me as though nothing had occurred, She only in silence reached down her hand, which I sought with both of mine, and said: "I am safe, thank God!" The horse, it appeared, had, on touching the ground, with one mighty leap regained the bank on my side of the ditch, and my wife had remained in the saddle, neither of them being hurt in the least. The whole was a work of a few seconds, and it seemed a miraculous deliverance.

In Osorno.

While awaiting letters from Valparaiso from our brethren there, I was not resting and folding my arms. I found Mr. R., the pastor, preparing for his return to Europe, and heard through him that another man would take his place, as he did not expect to return to this country. I began visiting the people, and found them in almost the same condition as those at the Lake. Mr. R. was a good man, but weak, and getting discouraged, he gave up the work and left the field. One day I visited a man who was confined to his room. He was glad that I had come, but when I spoke to him concerning Jesus and his soul, he became so angry that he opened the door and asked me to leave his house as quick as possible. He said: "I cannot bear to hear that name." I did not doubt it a moment, and I asked him to permit me to pray with him, and then I would go. The man had no desire to yield to my wish, but, opening my Bible, I began to read, and he shut the door; then I prayed earnestly for his soul. When I arose I saw the man's face looked terrible. I could not help but think of Cain when the Lord asked him: "Why is thy countenance fallen?" The man again stepped to the door, and said: "Please leave me; I cannot bear this." I deeply felt for the poor man, and thought, What will it be in the day of judgment, and is not this true, what the Lord of the living and the dead tells us concerning the rich man in hell? How will the unsaved — those who reject Christ on earth — bear the sight of the great white throne? not to speak of Him who sitteth thereon. How will they bear the songs of the redeemed — how bear the testimonies of the blood-washed throng? But last of all, how bear the memory of the past — the remembrance of never-returning opportunities, lost? When heaven and earth shall pass away at the sight, will they be able to resist that irresistible, sweeping force, and not be carried away to their eternal doom? Sin sinks into eternal misery. Away from God, — oh, what a hell!

A Mr. Worldly-wise said once to me: "Oh, this business of 'hell' has quit, — it's 'hades' now." I told him, if he did n't repent he would be permitted to live in "hades," when he sinks into hell. The question of choice would then, perhaps, not come up in his mind. But thanks be to God, while we live we may choose "to-day," and in Jesus we find power "this day," to fix our eternal destiny. What wondrous power!

> "O wondrous grace! O wondrous love!
> That called a Saviour from above
> To die on Calvary!"

Mr R. had left, and I applied for the church, and asked the privilege of preaching there. It was granted to me. A neighbor had lost a son by death. I visited the parents and found them quarrelling with God. They did not know Him, and so now quarrelled with Him. They had never sought to make His acquaintance, and yet they *knew* He was cruel and unjust. They had never read the Bible, but they *knew* it was untrue. They were left to themselves, and yet wondered that they were comfortless, and found themselves without a hope for their boy, without a hope for themselves. They *knew* everybody had to die except themselves. Oh, what wretchedness, what misery! It seems so hard to comfort here. They really need to see their sins in the light of the Gospel. They must know that they are lost, and hear that there is a Saviour — a way of salvation.

My First Funeral Sermon.

I was invited to officiate at the funeral, and I promised to bury the boy. I hoped that many of their friends would be present at the funeral, and that it might be an occasion of great blessing to the people. I was not mistaken, for a great many of those who were not accustomed to go to church, were present, and God led the discourse. I was much blessed, and the central question was put very pointedly, "How is it with thy soul?" and, "Prepare to meet thy God." Some left the grave before I had finished the preaching, and I saw they had left in anger. Amen. Others were thoughtful, and others, again, seemed convicted. I was not home long when a tall, heavy German entered my room, desiring to see me. The man seemed to be in a state of excitement, and I guessed what was up. He asked me how I dared to suppose that he was a sinner, and how I dared to talk at a funeral as though the people needed my discourse. I told him politely that really I thought the poor dead boy did n't need it, and would n't care whether I praised him or not, and that the occasion had been too solemn to think of talking only about the dead. "No man liveth to himself, and no man dieth to himself," and on these grounds I thought a lesson was to be derived for those remaining on earth.

The man began to curse, and swore frightfully at me; but the Lord kept me sweet. I made no more reply, and when he saw I did not get angry with him, he did not know what to do, and became rather confused. He looked like a man that had undertaken a manly job, and was not able to finish it. He was looking for a big quarrel — a fight — and an attempt on my part to throw him out doors; but no such thing occurred. The poor fellow was bitterly disappointed, and when in a friendly manner I asked him to take a seat, he turned to the door and left the house. But he felt still worse when he saw his friends, who had waited on the street for him, laughing at him, and saying, loud enough for me to hear it: "Well, we thought you'd eat the man alive, and here you are already!"

The man turned to see whether I had noticed this, and then, ashamed of himself, he silently disappeared, not caring for his friends.

I heard afterwards that he had intended to give me a good thrashing, and had boasted among his friends that he would do the job so well as to remove my desire for preaching the Gospel to the people. If these dear men would only fall out with themselves, it would help them, and discover to them their friends (?), who laugh at them when they get into trouble. Who will stick closer than a brother, or who is the "true Friend"? Friend may give his life for a friend, but to what profit? Only Jesus, dying, and while we were yet sinners, will save the soul. There is no real value in the death of any making such a sacrifice,— the glory of it fades away, as the grass that to-day is, and is cast into the fire to-morrow, — except the death of Jesus. At the sound of that story of the Cross, millions have found the salvation of a never-dying soul; at the sound of the story of a risen Jesus, millions have understood, "What is life?" At the sound of the mere mention of Jesus' name, millions have been thrilled, and the hopes that pass human knowledge and understanding, have been called to life within the soul, and have become tangible to the grasp of childlike faith; and a personal Holy Ghost has manifested Himself, showing us things to come.

"O 't is glory! O 't is glory!
O 't is glory in my soul!
I have touched the hem of His garment
And His power doth make me whole."

Persecution began also in this place. The people had not heard the truth, and had been permitted to go on in sin quite undisturbed. A man — one of the officials of the church — told me that I might have the church every Sunday, but I must cease preaching about sin and the Saviour. The other preacher had to comply with their wish, and I might as well do the same thing, if I meant to succeed. I asked the man: "What did your pastor preach, then?" "Oh, he told us to be good, but we didn't mind that much; he liked to enjoy himself as well as we did."

Now, I thought, as to the preaching, it is just what some others do in the pulpit — " telling the people to be good." That is about what some sermons amount to. I was not surprised to find the people in such a state of rebellion against God and his messenger. They had been playing at "sugar-coating," and now the "medicine," being applied to cure the disease, "cramped" their stomachs.

Preaching to Natives.

In the midst of these persecutions, the Lord converted my brother-in-law, who lay very sick with consumption. We earnestly prayed for him, and he rallied somewhat; and he said if God would restore him to health, he would yet go to study and preach the Gospel. He seemed to get much better, and he was so earnest that he said to me one day: "Let us go into the country and preach to the natives, and I will interpret for you." Accordingly we set out, and held several meetings in the neighborhood, and the people were much interested to hear the word, although they were severely reproved by the priests. But the Lord permitted the young man to sink back into his old disease, and he soon grew so weak that he could preach no longer. I had hoped that he would entirely recover his health, and become a worker in the Lord's vineyard.

Returning one Sabbath morning from a meeting with the natives, we met a number of wealthy Germans, who had gone out for a ride to the country. When they saw me, as they passed by, they cursed me. I thanked God for the grace that enabled me to offer silent prayer for those men. Seven years ago I probably should have challenged them to fight a duel, in German fashion. God wondrously saved me from anger when He removed the "roots of bitterness" — the moment He sanctified my soul, "through and through," and gave me the gift of perfect love.

Among the Children.

Now, I thought, the time had come that something should be done for the children, and accordingly I went out on the street — my wife and I — and invited them in, and these dear lambs learned to sing, and they enjoyed it so much. The Lord blessed me so with these children, that some of them would pray in their little gatherings, and in their way confess that they loved the Saviour. Oh, these hours with the children! How anxious they seemed to learn of Jesus! We had singing and prayer every afternoon for one hour, and the Bible-class on the Sabbath.

One day two little boys came to see me, and the younger one said: "Mr. K., I have a dollar here for you; will you take it?" I drew the boy towards me, and told him that I would take the money, providing he would tell me how he got it. The little fellow blushed, but could not say a word, — he looked confused, and, looking at his brother and me, he was tearing his finger-nails. Then I set him on my knee, and tried to persuade him to tell me all about it. It was a long time before he yielded, and it was when he saw that his brother was about to open his mouth to make the confession. He then told me, in his childish way, and I thought it was so sweet to listen to him (and it takes good boys to tell it alone): —

"My brother and I asked mother to let us cut some wood for the stove, one day, and we liked the work, and then I said to mother: 'Will you give us twenty-five cents if we cut an ox-cart full of wood?' Mother laughed, and said, 'Yes.' Now, when we had finished our lessons in the evening we run out into the wood and cut a little every day; but mother didn't know we cut much. Yesterday we asked ma to give us an oxcart and one of the farm hands, to bring in the wood that we cut; and we brought in four big loads. 'Mother,' we said, 'you must now give us a dollar, because there are four big loads'; but she wouldn't give us the money, because she thought we would spend it. We didn't want to tell ma what we wanted the money for; but she made us tell it, and I told her it was to be for the missionary.

Oh, that touched my heart, and I wept like a child. That was too much for me. I kissed the boys, and they ran out so full of joy. These were two boys of eight and twelve years, cutting wood to earn a dollar for the missionary! Praise the Lord! Surely the Lord was working among the children.

A young man came and asked me to give him a book to read. I gave him "Woltersdorf's Letters." Turning the leaves over carelessly, he asked whether there were any "nice stories" in it. I said that I remembered the time when I was about eighteen years old, when I sat down and shed tears over some idle tale — some novel — if it was written in some way affecting, and I liked it. Next I remembered the time when I read the story of God's love to man in sin, and I shed tears, and it saved my soul; while the former damned my soul. He took the book without asking questions.

On the first of November, I was invited out to the country to preach. We had a great blessing. One sister, seventy-nine years of age, came up to me after the preaching, and taking me by the hand, said: "I know now that I am the Lord's," and another younger sister said: "I have made a full step to the front." I had preached from Rev. ii. 10. It seemed that heaven was open, and we saw Jesus standing at the right hand of God.

On the way home, I desired much to see a family living near, and turning my horse, made my way toward the house. The head of the house had noticed my coming, and there were visitors at the house; and I was sorry to see they were drinking hard; I thought it best not to dismount, and waving my hand toward the party, turned to leave; but the whole party came to the door, bringing their drink with them; and at once insisted that I should drink with them, — just because they knew I did not use stimulants, nor drink water for mere pleasure. They sought a quarrel. I politely refused, when they poured out curses and swore awfully at me.

POLITE WITH DOGS.

The house-father then turned loose four large dogs, and excited them to take hold of me. I calmly bade them good-by, the dogs barking furiously, but not daring to touch me nor the horse, as I slowly rode off. People said they wondered that the dogs did not tear me in pieces; they were known to be dangerous animals. I understood it all right, for on another occasion a large dog confronted me, and taking off my hat, I politely bowed to Mr. Dog. He growled, and, completely overcome, retired to one side, but steadily looked after me until I was out of sight. Now I do think we try to treat men — our enemies — a little better when we are filled with the Holy Spirit; and our behavior, while they are raging, will strike them something like a new idea, and before they recover, the steam is blown off.

"The servant is not above his Master; but every one that is perfect shall be as his Master." This is a word of which we might say: "Lo, now dost thou speak plainly." More like Him — be "as his Master. A man who professed to know the Lord," said to me he did not believe it right to go to God in prayer for every "little thing." I told him the very hairs of our head were numbered, and not one of them is left unnoticed, and asked him whether he did not think that a hair was rather a small affair? When the Lord washes the heart, he levels our head, to be sure, and the whole man, with everything belonging to him, is under supervision of the Holy Ghost. However, some people, I find, are great men — great women — and only deal wholesale; but they find that the scales turn on them, and the Lord does n't mind "these little things."

Now when the work among the children began to be noticed, the teachers began their work of pulling down what was built up. They abused the children at school for attending the meetings, and at last succeeded in causing the parents to forbid their coming to me. Most of the parents of those attending the Sunday-school were ungodly, and soon only the two little wood-cutters remained — both parents being godly people.

By this time, I needed a new suit of clothing, and I talked to God about it, and said that in His infinite goodness He might provide me with necessary garments. My father-in-law, if he had known anything about it, would have at once responded; but this I did not want. The Lord had led me to depend on Him, and I let the matter rest in His hands. We had an old stove which we had used at the Lake, and a young man had heard of it, and came to inquire whether we would sell it. I had not thought that any one would buy the stove, as it was in somewhat defective condition. I told him what I thought, but he insisted on having it, and so I showed it to him, and especially the broken parts. He said he would take the stove and repair it, and handing me $17, said he had taken that amount with him, and that I was welcome to it. The following Sabbath, after the preaching at our house, a sister took me aside, and placing $20 in my hand, said: "A person not wishing to be known, sends you this." I had never intimated to any one, by a word, that I had need of anything,—except to God,—and never until now had I received any assistance in money to this amount from anybody, with the exception of the dollar from the two boys. So the Lord supplied my need, and to Him belonged all the glory. Praise His name! The cloth was then bought, and a tailor came to the house and there made the suit for me. Some people are so "God-fearing," as to be afraid to trust God with their wants. The Lord have pity on us! The Lord answers prayer.

The following Sabbath I was invited to preach five miles south of Osorno. A good number were present. I preached from Heb. i. 1–3. God graciously manifested Himself to some present, and some entered into life, while some were hardened. Oh, the terrible infidelity of these Germans is heart-sickening! But had I not been there myself? Has not the power of Jesus reached even me? My soul, wait thou upon God: thou shalt yet see thy desire.

On my way home, a German accompanied me, also on horseback, who was very angry that I went about preaching the word of God; and being exceedingly mad against me, used frightful language. In my heart I prayed for the man, and he was the more angry when he saw me patiently riding along; and then, shaking his fist in my face, put spurs to his horse, and crying out: "You are a fool!" dashed away, out of sight. I remember that man's face well, distorted with rage, only because he had heard the truth, and it had struck him to the heart; and with all his might — Satan helping him — he shook off the conviction for sin. Somehow, some one would always get mad; but, thanks be to God! some always found the Saviour. The men were terribly steeped in sin and crime, and shameless before their wives and children; but, alas! in many instances, the wife and even small children were as bad, in a way I had never witnessed elsewhere. I praised God that He counted me worthy to suffer for His name's sake. Thus the armor is kept bright and grace abounds. Glory to God for the perfect love in my soul!

This same man had been sick, nigh unto death, only two weeks ago. He desired me then to pray for him. He seemed as meek as a lamb, but the Lord had spared his life, and he had forgotten the mercy of God, and broken his vow, — and how many are doing just the same thing? Faith, hope, charity; but the greatest is charity. No wonder, then, the Lord practices it on man, — it conquers the world, — it has conquered me.

About this time we had a visit from Bro. Hoffman. His work at the Lake was hard, and he suffered much persecution. On one occasion their life was in danger.

While riding with his wife to an appointment, several young men tried to run over them while they were riding close to a precipice; but when they caught hold of the horse's bridle, it broke, and the horses of the men were suddenly frightened and ran away with them. They were pursued and one of them arrested; but soon released without a hearing. The reason of this mad attempt seemed to be: the Lord had converted a Roman family. Every member of the household had been soundly converted, and all bore faithful testimony to the saving power of God. Formerly this family served so faithfully in the ranks of the enemy, that they had gotten quite a reputation, and of course the devil would not be quiet about it; but it was done — the great transaction was done — although Satan raged, and Bro. H. was willing to suffer.

I received no news as yet from Valparaiso, and here there was no abiding place for me. The new preacher from Germany was soon expected to arrive. The time spent here has been rich in experience, and several persons have found the Saviour.

CHAPTER VIII.

MY CALL TO VALPARAISO.—LEAVING THE COLONIES.

I CONCLUDED to go up to Valparaiso without awaiting an answer. I prayed and fasted about the matter, and it appeared clear that it was the will of God that I should go. The witness was given me so clearly, that not a thought of a doubt was admitted. Once more I visited the Lake, and with Bro. Hoffman was privileged to preach several times to the people there. I found the Lord had wonderfully blessed Bro. Hoffman, and I heard many precious testimonies from the young people. I met that family which had so recently been converted to God. They were truly all the Lord's, and sound in their testimony. The persecutions had intensified, and in the midst of all, these tender plants grew beautifully, to the glory of the wonderful Jesus. I soon returned to Osorno, and leaving my dear wife with her parents, started for Valparaiso.

On Christmas day, at noon, I arrived in Valparaiso. There I met the Rev. Mr. Jeffrey, who was preaching to the seamen. He was not very well, and he invited me to preach for him on the following Sabbath on board the bark *La Querida.* This was my first sermon to seamen, and the Lord put His seal to the word, and blessed us all. I began to love the seamen from the first day that I spent with them. In the afternoon I visited six ships, and gathered the men in the forecastle for the occasion, and there spoke to them. Singing and prayer followed. These dear sailors enjoyed the meetings very much, and when I asked them about their souls' welfare, they manifested a desire to seek the Lord, and asked me to come back.

On Sunday, the fourth of January, I gathered a German congregation, and preached to them from Matt. xxii. 42. On the twenty-second of January, our Annual Conference was held at Santiago, and I proceeded thither to meet the workers who had come to the West Coast of South America under William Taylor. There were present: Prof. Wright and Miss Lelia Waterhouse, of Concepcion; L. C. Smith and Miss Vassbinder, of Copiapo; Mr. La Fetra, Santiago; Mr. and Mrs. Jeffrey, Mr. and Mrs. Collyer, and von Barchwitz-Krauser, all of Valparaiso. Mr. Collyer had been working at Iquique, but the war between Chili and Peru had broken out, and he was compelled to leave the field. (He filled the pulpit of Dr. Trumbull while this gentleman was visiting the United States.) There were others on the coast, who had not been able to come — the distance being so great.

We received news that Prof. Humphrey and wife,

would shortly be compelled to leave Tacna, Peru, on account of the war, and also that Mr. Magnus Smith, of Mollendo, Peru, had died, and Mrs. Smith had returned to the States. Bro. Birdsall had passed away some time ago, at Aspinwall. So ten workers met at this, our first Conference. All had passed through the fire but our spirits were bright, and the prospects encouraging for those who had set their heart to work faithfully. The school-work was chiefly among the natives

It was now decided that Mr. Jeffrey, of Valparaiso, should be transferred to Concepcion, to enter school-work, as his health had failed in Valparaiso, and his services were required at the school at Concepcion. I had already labored a few weeks in Valparaiso, and to my great joy, I had found that much work was to be done; but with the seamen on shore I had met with stout resistance, on the part of those who kept those dens of vice which characterize the seaports in all parts of the world, and I did not see my way clear how to approach them and do an effectual work. The work was completely new to me, and although I experienced no fear whatever, yet I felt a lack of proper understanding as to how such a work might be carried on, and I also confounded this with a sense of unfitness for that peculiar work; for I seemed to see clearly what was necessary, in one sense, and yet there was a cloud. I told the brethren about my convictions, and they decided to send Bro. Jeffrey down to Valparaiso, and ask the committee of the Seamen's Society as to my fitness, and bring up the report. The report came, and was about as follows: "We want Bro. K. for the seamen's work, and think he is the man; only — he preaches too much holiness." The old sore of the church.

Good Common Sense.

But Bro. LaFetra said: "Probably that is the reason why he is the man, and why success has marked his labors among the seamen already." All, with one voice, said then: "Go on, Bro. Krauser, — preach as the Lord shall lead you. Amen. Praise the Lord!" Then three beside me went to an upper room, and there prayed to God to lead and bless me in the work, and show me what to do to strike the proper blow, and do a God-glorifying work among the seamen on shore and in the bay.

While thus praying with my dear brethren, the light came, and I could see what the Lord wanted me to do. It was clear to me that the very strongholds of Satan must be assailed, and undermined by prayer, until they should fall and crumble to dust. I arose and said with a loud voice: "Here, Lord, am I: send me," and then a baptism fell on me, such as I had not experienced before, and it abode with me.

When I came down and joined the other brethren, I

walked to and fro in the room, weeping and laughing, and clapping my hands. I felt the Lord would do a work in Valparaiso, and He had just given me the strength to do it in His name. I received there a special baptism for a special work.

The day drew nigh when we all should separate, each one to his field of labor. It had done us good to be thus permitted to meet and commune with each other; and, much strengthened, we parted, to enter upon our work for the Master.

CHAPTER IX.

A RICH MINE DISCOVERED. — GOING TO WORK.

My first work was — true to my conviction — to go to one of the saloon-keepers, who kept one of the worst dens in the place, — he was a German, himself a hard drinker, and also a drunkard-maker, — and ask him to permit me to visit his saloon every Sunday afternoon, and hold a prayer-meeting with the men whom I would find in the place. The Lord was with me when I entered the house, and then the moment came when I put the question fairly before him. The man looked at me first as though he thought I was joking; but when I repeated the question, he could be no longer in doubt that I meant business, and then replied: "Well, Mr. Krauser, I believe you don't know what you are talking about." Then I began to plead with the man as my soul would plead for the soul of a poor lost sinner at the throne of grace. I asked the man whether he had never taken pity on those young men, or felt for them, when at his bar they would spend their last hard-earned dollar, and then he would see them stagger out on the street, mad with drink; and how, in many cases, he had to throw them out by force; and whether he had ever thought that so many sailor-boys had dear praying mothers, wives, and children, at home? He replied to all this: "Oh, well, business is business. I have nothing to do with all that; but for you to come here and hold meetings, I don't see that you will accomplish much, except to ruin my business." My heart went out after the dear seamen, and with tears I begged the man to give me a chance in his house, to pray with the men, and to permit me to go in and out as I liked. He could not resist now, any more; but turning half aside, said: "Well, all right; come on."

Oh, how my soul was filled with thanksgiving toward God! The words of the man seemed like music to the ear. I thanked him heartily, and told him that I expected God would bless him, too.

My next business was to get another place like it in some other street. I felt that the banner must be raised right in the lion's den, and God gave me grace to go and conquer. I soon found the place I wanted — a large boarding-house — kept by a Swede, who probably did the best business in the line of dealing out death to poor sailors. He kept several "runners" to decoy sailors on shore and strip them of everything they possessed, and then throw them on the "beach." This sort of men are best known among sailors as "land-sharks."

I called for the proprietor, who received me kindly, but when I told him my errand, he began to give me a lecture to this effect, that it was no use to try to do anything for sailors; Jack would always be a "bad egg," and the best thing I could do for them would be to let them alone. A fine lecture for the devil's pocket — it did all honor to the trade; but I was not inclined to give it up quite so fast. The man was a good talker, and I confess I did not like him half so well as my other friend in saloon No. 1. However, he consented at last, but in a room up stairs — not in the bar-room; yet I could visit the bar-room as often as I wished; but if he did n't like it any longer, I would have to give it up. I knew he would not like it very long; but I accepted the arrangement.

Thus I had fixed my Sunday work. Preaching in the morning from 10 to 11, in German, on shore. From 11.30, in the bay, among the seamen. Afternoon from 2 to 3, in saloon No. 1, and from 3 to 6, visiting the crews on board ship in the bay; and in the evening, from 7 to 8, in saloon No. 2. Three times during the week, in the evenings, visit all the drinking-saloons, dancing halls, and brothels, and twice each week, in the evening, to hold a prayer-meeting in the bay, on board ship. This plan was made to be followed for an indefinite time, so that changes could be admitted to suit the circumstances, and to suit the development of the work. Besides, every fortnight, I engaged to preach at the English hospital, and to drop an hour out of my visits to the bay, on those days. It was plain enough that this was my work, and that less could not be done if I expected results, and the Lord would give me health and strength. I felt this in every drop of blood running through my veins. My soul was filled with God, and the baptism for work was upon me.

Prayer-Meeting in a Bar-room.

Sunday, the 25th, I held my first meeting in bar-room No. 1. Being Sunday, there were a good many present. I went into the adjoining card-room, and invited all to attend. This first meeting was conducted without much disturbance on the part of those who were intoxicated. Some laughed while prayer was offered, but when we sang the hymns, there was silence, and most of those present were soon engaged in singing. Then followed an earnest exhortation, and prayer in closing. The impression was profound, and in the eyes of some of the men there were tears. I spoke with several about their souls, and found that some had been wounded by the Spirit.

In the afternoon I visited eight ships, and spoke to about sixty men. At 7 P. M., saloon No. 2 was visited. I first gathered the men into the bar-room and then invited them to come up stairs. The proprietor did not like that. He said he had to live, and business was business. I turned to the men and said: "You see this man cares not for your welfare — only for your money. It does not matter to him what becomes of you, if he only can get your money. Now he has the devil helping him in this; but you have God to help you; if you will let Him, He will save your souls from sin, and give you something that will remain with you forever — His Holy Spirit. You here partake of these ardent spirits. They will stay with you while you indulge, and then influence you to all manner of sin and crime, and craze your brain; while your wife and children, and a poor mother, long for a penny to buy bread, and your children need shoes to their bare feet." Thus I spoke in the bar-room to them, while they listened. I knew the bar-keeper well enough. Those talkative fellows stand a great deal; and thinking they are a great deal wiser after all, let me have my say out, and think: "I'll put him out some other time." In the meantime the Gospel is preached. Then I spoke to those men up in their rooms, and prayed with them. We had a blessed season this day, and God be praised. Amen.

I shall now follow the line of general development of the blessed work that soon followed in this city, and not report every meeting in order; but select from my journal only such points as will be of interest to the reader, and are calculated to help, and also to glorify God, as well as give a clear idea as to the work that has been accomplished within the three years from 1880, to February, 1884.

The meetings in the saloons were wonderfully blessed, but more or less persecution arose as the work of soul-saving began to show. The third Sabbath in saloon No. 1, showed that by this time the devil had been fairly aroused. While praying with those who would kneel with me, others would strike the table with their fists, and pour out their beer about me and curse and swear in the most awful manner; but still, in the midst of all this, some sailor would shed tears of repentance, and in all the noise among drunken comrades, plead with God and receive pardon; and then some would go out with me, and help me in the work, and bear testimony to the saving power of Jesus. Saloon-keeper No. 2, now forbade my coming to the place any longer. He said it hurt his business; but I told him I must come, even though he should take the room from me. He did that; but then I visited the bar-room and distributed tracts. When I came in he went out, and did not come back until I had left the place. The poor man hated to see me, but had not the power to forbid me his house.

Shot Behind the Counter.

In saloon No. 1, a man — one of the runners — was shot dead behind the bar; but now the Lord had taken hold of the man who kept this terrible place. When he came and begged me to bury the man, I took him aside and prayed with him. I told him about the judgment to come, and about the love of God, and that Jesus had died for him. I also told him, if he did not give up his house soon, the Lord would visit upon him the blood of the many victims that had lost body and soul in his place, and through his influence for evil. The man seemed really broken, and I rejoiced to see it. Oh, that God might give that man grace to give his heart to Jesus, and close that den of vice, and find something better to do to earn his bread.

A number of saloon-keepers, who probably had not heard the word of God from the pulpit from their boyhood, were there, and the Lord anointed me for the occasion. The bitter past rose up before them, and many wished for a moment they were not there to hear it. But it was the solemn truth — the word of God declared the truth. I spoke with many after the body had been deposited, and poor Mr. B., the saloon-keeper, had a hard time to rid himself of conviction, and for the first time he promised to think of these things that he had heard of late.

The following Sunday I had the great joy to see a sailor on board an American ship converted to God, and two others earnestly seeking the Lord. Our meeting in saloon No. 1, in the afternoon, was rather a peculiar one. While I was praying, and several others of the men had knelt down with me, the gambling and drinking was going on at the very table around which we bowed. The men playing did not feel inclined to stop, and one threatened to make it hot for me if I did not leave the place; and although he shook his fist in my face, he was prevented from striking me, and I prayed on. It was a wonderful meeting, and before we had finished our knee-work there was silence in the room. The worst crier had suddenly left. Truly the ungodly shall not be able to stand in the congregation of the righteous.

The whole neighborhood in this part of the city had been wonderfully stirred, for the Lord had raised up several men from among the offscouring of society, and soundly converted them, and these helped me nobly in the work. A little band of four saved men, who had been picked out of the gutter, accompanied me to all the gambling hells and brothels in the parts most frequented by sailors and mechanics, and other foreigners living in the city. A hand-to-hand fight now commenced, and Satan was well stirred up, and tried to rally his host against me; but in every battle we came out more than conquerors.

Collared by a Woman.

In my visits during the week to those dens, I stepped into one saloon, kept by a very tall and strong native women. The place was crowded by foreigners and natives. I called in and sat down among them, and began to distribute my tracts, when suddenly I felt some one take me by the collar from behind, and very unceremoniously raised me to my feet and marched me to the door, giving me a lift which landed me across the pavement on the street. The good woman of the house had managed to do all that in a very short time; but I was not to be baffled like that, and a second time I came to the door, but the woman, in great anger, met me again, and told me if I stepped across the threshold she would strike me in the face. I then drew out some Spanish tracts, and handing them to her, said that they contained the story of Jesus, and the word of life. She pushed the hand that offered the tracts aside, and pushing me back — for I had advanced while talking towards the interior of the room — she again threatened to throw me out on the street. Then I said: "Well, if you throw me out at the front door I shall come in at the back, for I must talk to these men inside." The face of the woman changed into a smile. I never saw anything done so quick, and I marched in, and handed her the Spanish tracts, which were no longer refused. I sat down with the men at the tables, and, unmolested, I was permitted to read my Bible, and talk to the men. They had hoped first that I would be frightened by the woman, and run; but soon found themselves in a very tight place, for on such occasions the truth, and only the whole truth, was fearlessly proclaimed. Their open sins and their secret sins were laid open to their minds; but I never left any men without I could see the Spirit's work that was going on in their hearts. Before leaving the place, I told the woman who kept it, to give her heart to Jesus, and told her about the women who clustered about the cross of Jesus on the day of His crucifixion, and tried to show her what a noble stand they had taken, and yet she, lost and ruined herself, was taking her stand against this Christ, and trying to ruin others. She listened most attentively. The poor woman had probably never heard anything of Christ before. She then told me I could come back whenever I liked, and promised never to throw me out doors again. I said, Amen! and departed.

That same evening I made arrangement for a nice large room, which I rented for religious meetings, right in the centre of a great many saloons and gambling hells, — beautifully located for a soul-saving work; and the following day I organized a "fellowship band," and in the name of God we would go forth to conquer or die. The saloon-keepers and gamblers and brothel-keepers had united to "kill us out," and under all circumstances, frustrate our designs; for they had found business was growing worse, and their best customers were getting converted, and not only that, but they had lost one of their number, who had just enlisted to fight under the banner of Jesus, and some three others had to close up their saloons for want of customers; for no foreigner or native was sure that he would not somewhere meet " that confounded parson," as they used to say, and be reproved for their sins. Yes, praise God! the time had come when they felt ashamed to be seen about these places, or even in that quarter of the city, which had become a pest to the community.

The Maintop.

This part of the city was known to seamen, and to all pleasure-seeking people, under the name of " The maintop." For the last forty years Satan had reigned here, and no one had ever dared to dispute his rights.

Our little band now consisted of ten God-fearing young men. One of them — my assistant leader — used to be called by his former shipmates " the ship's devil." He had been a drunkard, and steeped head over heels in sin and vice, and now, just as faithful, served his new-found Master, whom he now loved with all his heart and with all his soul.

How God Saved a Rumseller.

Another of the number had kept a brothel for twenty-two years; but when I had visited his saloon every week several times, and finding he somehow could never succeed in keeping me away, he concluded to lock the door whenever I should come near; but he could not bar out the Spirit of God, and so I prayed now especially for his poor soul on the outside. This troubled him so, that one night he came to our mission-room, close by, and after meeting stayed until 10 o'clock pleading with God to free him from his business. The poor fellow made a mistake here. He was afraid he would have no bread and butter, and yet he knew he would be eternally lost if he carried on his pernicious trade. I tried to point him to Jesus, as he laid on the floor, rolling in agony. I told him to tell Jesus about his sins, and first obtain forgiveness, and the way for his daily bread would open before him — God would take care of that. He could not see it yet, and he went away that night unsaved. But some of the noble band united that same night with me in prayer, and we claimed that man's soul for heaven, and left him there, — we were looking forward to God to deliver the poor man from sin. How I wept with him! I think I never beheld such a picture of misery in all my life before. He had ruined himself, almost, through drink, and he was very weak in body, and Satan seemed to claim him for hell. The struggle had been severe, and yet no deliverance.

The next day I found his saloon closed, and on inquiry could get no clue as to where the man was. This was a great trial to me, but I was much relieved in prayer, and I felt certain the man was in God's hand,

and He would see to him. Three days after, this man appeared at our meeting in the mission-room, leaning on a cane, and looking very sick. But his face looked different, and his eyes shone as he stood up to tell us " his experience." "That night, when I left you," he said, "I had not found peace, but I had given up the cup, which has, as it appears, almost killed me, for I am consumptive, and do not expect to live very long. During the night I took very sick, and in the morning I was unable to open the saloon. Then I prayed to God in some way to deliver me, and rather to let me die than to let me go into my business again. That moment I could give up everything, including myself, and quick as thought I felt and knew my sins had passed away. I do not know how long I prayed, but it seemed I could not stop praising God. I then sent for my family; told my wife what God had done for me, and that the saloon was to remain closed, and never to be opened again. I was now feeling worse, and was taken home, and had to go to bed. I thought God would take me away; but He has spared me to tell you what Christ has done for me. This morning I felt strong enough to leave my bed, and I also know that when I am strong enough I shall have work to support my family, for a wholesale house in town offered me this afternoon a situation as store-house keeper, and they will wait until I am strong."

This was his own testimony, and what a meeting followed now! Truly, God had not only saved that man, but also sent him there that night to our meeting.

A Remarkable Conversion.

A young man whom I had met in the street as he was just going to step into a saloon, and invited him to this meeting, was so convicted of sin, that he could not leave the room, and desired that we should pray with him. We stayed with the young man an hour, and no light had come to his poor soul. I could not understand, and moving up to him I was led to say, "My poor friend, you must be keeping back something from the Lord, or else you would be saved. Tell me what it is, and God may help me to say something to you." He had a hard struggle, but drawing me close up to him, he said: "Mr. Krauser, you do n't know what a sinner I am, and how shamefully I have sinned against God and myself. I cannot give myself to God and be a Christian this evening. Oh, if I was well, I might, but now I can't — I can't!" I begged him to tell me what was wrong. "You must be cut loose from the power of darkness this evening; you cannot trust yourself to leave this room without your Saviour, or you will fall deeper than ever." He then told me: "Mr. Krauser, I have a terrible disease upon me, and I will be compelled to go to the hospital to-morrow. How can I expect that Christ will receive me in this condition, and what will those at the hospital, and my friends say, if I make a profession? They will laugh at me and call me a hypocrite."

Indeed, I felt that Christ must manifest Himself in a special manner in this case. The fact that this man could be saved, and that Jesus would never turn him away, although he came "ruined by the fall," was plain to me, and I told him Jesus only could and would save just now, if he was in earnest about his soul, and would believe Christ's invitation as to the "whosoever" and the "to-day, if you will hear His voice, harden not your heart." Christ had saved a seven-devilled Mary; Christ would not forsake him in the hour of his greatest need.

The young man rallied himself, and cried aloud: "Yes, Lord, I will believe!"

Oh, that hour was precious! No one can ever forget the sight which our eyes beheld, the moment the soul, chained down by Satan by the power of terrible sin, burst the fetters by faith in Jesus, and triumphantly rose, a pardoned man. Tears of joy burst from his eyes, and how could we keep from weeping? Not an eye was dry in the room, and truly the angels rejoiced over a sinner that returned to the Father's house in deep penitence, but believing — taking God at His word. The new-born brother then told us that he had been brought up in the Roman Church, and that all his people belonged to that church; "but," said he, "oh that they might find this same Jesus! They are all unsaved."

Good for a Beginning.

Now provision could be made for my dear wife to come up to Valparaiso. A friend gave me the passage money, and I sent it to Osorno, and we met. However, our income was very small, and I had not been able to buy any furniture. We had sufficient bedding, however, and so could make our bed upon the bare floor, and trusted God in due season to give us a bedstead, and such other furniture as we needed. By faith we rented a house, — it looked rather empty, and the rent very high, — but our hearts were full of God, and we knew our Heavenly Father was rich, and with Him we rested all our wants. Means for our temporal support were coming in freely. The secretary of the Seaman's Mission received from all who would freely contribute, and my German congregation did all they could. Sometimes the secretary would run behind in the amount, but some one would always make up the necessary sum, and never lacked we anything. When God gave us a standing, we could get some furniture, to the amount of $180, and take our time to pay it. We did this in faith, for we believed God would send us the amount above our daily necessities. We were also able to spare a few rooms in the house; and prayed the Lord to send us two good young men, who, in a few days after rented the rooms, and thus furnished us the means to help paying a rent of $55 per month.

NATIVE WORK.

My wife then concluded to accompany me in my work. While I visited the men in the "maintop," she did the work among the females; but when she had obtained permission to hold her meetings in a room every Sunday, not only females attended, but also the men crowded the place. These meetings were purely among the natives, and in the Spanish language. God wonderfully blessed the natives of that locality. The women would bring pieces of carpet, which they used to kneel on when in their Roman temples they bowed before an image, or at the confessional chair; and eagerly desired that the preacher should stand or kneel on the rugs. It showed a good spirit, and the hunger and thirst after the word of God increased, and some were led into the light, and spoke openly in the meetings. One evening, five saloon-keepers attended our meeting at the room, having come to disturb the assembly. They kept up the noise while I was preaching, but I suddenly stopped and said: "Now, friends, I will show you that I can make a greater noise than you can, — just let me have a chance and see." I got their attention completely, and God blessed me in a message directly addressed to these five men, and at the close I asked all to get on their knees and pray to God. The members of the band present understood the work, and while I prayed, dispersed among those assembled, and began their "asking the question," and praying with those five saloon-keepers. Everybody was on their knees, and one of the saloon-keepers cried like a child. He said he didn't know what had happened to him.

A Native Converted.

One native, who spoke a little English, had come in, and began in a stammering tongue and in broken language to pray to God for the forgiveness of his sins; and soon there was such a noise of voices in the room, that with a hearty amen, I closed my prayer, arose, and closed the door that led out on the street, and helped to work among the seekers, for there were about eight crying for mercy. When I went to close the door, a Church of England minister, who had desired to see something of the work, and had attended that very meeting, rose and said: "Well, Bro. Krauser, let me out first. God is with you, and I think you can carry the meeting to a close. I'll go home." When he had left, I could not repress the thought arising: The good brother thought he got into a hot place. Certainly he thought the meeting got quite "out of order"; and meeting him afterward, he murmured something about "order," "noise," "excitement," and those usual complaints of the "orderly" class; but he was a good man and rejoiced when he heard that the Lord that night had saved five precious souls! He only said: "Well, now, five souls! You'd better be careful." Now, these good ministerial brethren let me work, but stayed away, but then I think they had plenty of work to do. They sympathized truly, and helped to raise money to carry on the work.

The Priests After Me.

But now the old enemy, Satan, sent a priest to trouble us. The house where we rented our room, belonged to one of his lambs, and we were told to leave at once. There was no use to say a word against it. We must leave immediately, for the priest, Mr. ———, had threatened that he would not receive her confession, and would not grant her absolution; and the poor woman, the owner of the house, was frightened so much that she dare not permit us to stay any longer. The Lord had a better plan for us, only we did not know it at that time; so we thought it a hard trial, on account of the souls that were daily being ensnared by Satan. But who could be more concerned than the Lord Himself? and we prayed to the Lord for a better place.

The preparations for removal were commenced the

following day. Some of "the boys" were to help me take away the benches, tables, lamps and books; and walking up the street toward the house, we saw, a little farther ahead, a woman who had kept a house of ill-fame, of the lowest order, vacating her place — moving her trunks out. I went up to see what was going on. Seeing me stand there, she came up and said: "I have concluded to give up the business, and think it's time to think of something better. I'll try to take in washing, and earn a living that way." I took her by the hand and said: "God bless you, and help you to become a Christian woman!" She said that she would try. I had often prayed in that house with the inmates, and taken out many young men and brought them over to the mission-room, and some had been converted to God. But this woman was very talkative, and I could have no confidence in anything she said or promised. At times she would even speak as though she was a Christian, and a very good woman. I considered her quite a dangerous person, and remarkably gifted to allure young men to her den of infamy; and I really believe it was no sincerity that led her to give up the house, but rather the "hard times," as some called the slack in business since the "missionary" had come around. She gave me the address of the owner of the house, and running back to my boys, I told them to stop moving and wait till I would return, and that I had found the "better place," and that I was on my way to rent a large front room, leading directly to the street, in the house formerly occupied by Mrs. ——.

CHAPTER X.

IN THE HOT-BED OF VICE AND CRIME.

IN an hour the arrangements were completed, and our furniture removed to the new room. Things looked rather dirty inside, and four of us set immediately to work, and before sweeping up, each member of the band contributed a little money, and sufficient paper was bought to nicely paper the room. I got an apron, cut the paper, and while one of the brethren swept the walls, another pasted the paper, and I tried my hand at paper-hanging, in which I succeeded admirably. Then we all set to scrubbing the floor, and soon the place looked clean and smelled sweet. "Bless the Lord!" we all said, when we had finished our task. Never did work seem so sweet before. Then a brother in the gas-fitting business came, when he heard we had got a large new room, and presented us with a gas-meter, pipes, and two chandeliers, to throw light on the subject; and in three days afterward we dedicated and opened our room. In the meantime I visited the saloons and the shipping, and held prayer-meetings there; and wherever I found an audience I preached to them. Only one of the five rum-sellers who a few days ago attended the meeting at the old place, was brought to God that night; and another promised to give up his dancing-house. However, a week after that, I found him still engaged in the same business, and I waited for the usual dancing evening, on Thursday, when I expected to have an opportunity to speak to such people. The dancing-room was crowded. Natives and foreigners were present — mechanics and seamen.

Dancing-House Proprietor in Close Quarters.

When I came in the rum-seller tried to avoid me; but I walked right up to him, and asked his permission to read, sing, and pray with the crowd. He looked desperate, and said: "Oh, please let us alone, here! this is no place for meeting now, and if you attempt to disturb the dance, you'll get killed here to-night." The crowd looked to be a rather wild sort. There were many intoxicated seamen, behaving themselves more like brutes than human beings. The rum-seller himself thought he had a rough set there that night, and he called my attention to the fact. "Now, you know very well I don't mind that," I said, "and if you just consent, it will be all right. Don't you pity these poor fellows?" I went on to say, "and haven't you done harm enough in this place? How can you dare turn me away like that? I've got more right here than you, and more right than the devil who damns these souls to hell.

God wants to save these harlots, gamblers, blasphemers, and drunkards; yes, God wants to save you, too. Are you not ashamed to send me away? Now come, my good friend, let me shake your strong hand; just see these hard hands! Ah, yes, you used to work once with these strong hands, and in the sweat of your brow, and bread tasted sweet, then; but oh, to-day it is so very different, and so much different now from the days when you were quite a little boy, and your dear mother used to take you up on her lap, and folded your little hands. They were clean, then, and innocent, and she taught you to pray 'Our Father, which art in heaven.'"
I looked at him, and tried to catch his eye. The poor fellow was quite broken up, now, and he gently said: "Go on, Mr. Krauser, I know you are right; I can't refuse you."

Thankful to my Redeemer, and my soul filled with wondrous love, I turned toward the assembly, and began singing a hymn. They instantly stopped the music and the dancing, and the deafening noise ceased to be. For a few moments they were awe-struck, and stood staring at me; but then a drunken sailor broke the silence, and breaking out in curses, advanced toward me and caught my arm, and like a rag he began whirling me round in the middle of the room, and then, with an oath, he let me go suddenly, and I shot across the hall into the next corner, and landed squarely on a chair.

Everybody was in an uproar of laughter, and they thought it was great fun, and now they watched me to see what I would do next. But I did not stir. I felt as sweet as ever, and remaining right where I was, comfortably seated on a chair, and finishing the hymn, I opened the Bible, which had not fallen from my grasp in the rather unsought-for exercise, and was about to begin to read. Again there was a few seconds of silence; but now my friend got fairly mad, and, coming toward me to get hold of me once more, he was confronted by another seaman, who placed himself at that instant between me and the assailant. Clinching his big fist, he shouted: "Who dares touch this man, has to come this way first! Don't you know he is a minister? Now dare, if you will! I don't think it will do us any harm to listen to what he will say." I arose now and said to the two men before me: "I am glad to see you are both so courageous, and I'm sure you won't be afraid if I now tell you what God says about poor sinners in this book, and how he loves them. Just sit down, all of you, and then I'll go on." Everybody obeyed, and a pin might be heard to fall on the floor.

How to Manage.

"Now, let's have a good hymn. I know sailor-boys like to sing. Let's have a sailor's hymn — old Sankey's hymn — 'Pull for the shore, sailor, pull for the shore!'

The whole crowd joined in, and the voices were strong and clear. Then I told them of Jesus and His love, and I told them of a young man who used to visit here, and whom some of them knew, and said: "Now, you don't know what has become of poor Wickliff. I'll tell you. I met him at the hospital the other day, and now he's dead. I watched him pass over the river; but he didn't talk any more as he used to. You know he often attended our meetings down in the room, and he would n't give up his sins; he didn't want to give you up, and he kept on sticking to you, and got drunk with you nearly every night, until you saw him walk about like a shadow, dirty and sick, and you deserted him, and tried to forget him. But Wickliff told me his story before he died. He raised himself up in his bed and told me to come up closer. He said: 'Mr. Krauser, I am going to die, and I am only twenty-two years old.' He hid his face in his hands, and then wept bitterly. What do you suppose the poor boy remembered? I think his lost young life rose up before him. He then bent over to me and whispered, 'My mother!' Ah, that was it. 'My mother!' he repeated, and then tears choked his voice. My boys, do you remember a mother to-night? I wonder whether Wickliff's mother ever prayed with him. That was just what was the matter. He went on, then, and said: 'My mother used to pray for me. I could not stand it, and I ran away. But I wrote her I would send her money, for I knew she depended on me for a living. I never sent her any, I spent it all in drink, and now I'm here dying. I have killed myself.' He hid his face again and cried. I told Wickliff about Jesus, and I saw how he stretched out his feeble hands, and cried: 'O Jesus, save me, a poor sinner! don't let me die and be lost!' God answered his prayer before he passed away, and he said, when he could scarcely whisper, 'Jesus, blessed Jesus! Yes, Jesus saves me now!' Only one bitter thought rose up once more. He said: 'Only twenty-two years — all lost!' Then he passed over. God has taken him; you will never see him more, unless you prepare for heaven. God save you all; let us pray, and get down on our knees, and you cry out to God to have mercy on you, miserable sinners. You will die in your sins if you don't."

There were no dry eyes in that strange assembly, and while I prayed, many sighs and groans were heard, and then many came down to the meeting-room with me when I quitted the place, and some there found the Saviour.

Two days after this meeting, the dancing-house was no more; and visiting the boiler-works soon after, and while among the workmen distributing tracts, whom should I find but my tall American, who kept that dancing-house. I took him by the hand, and looking straight at him, asked: "And how tastes the bread now?" "Oh, much sweeter, really, I assure you." "Have you given your heart to Jesus?" "No, but I hope to find Him yet."

Attempt to Cut His Throat.

At our meeting one evening, a man came and said: "I have been a drunkard for eight years, and have had the delirium tremens thrice. Last Sunday I was arrested at the moment when I had placed the razor to my throat, to cut it from ear to ear. I have just been released again, and I heard the singing in this place, and now my mind is quite made up, not to leave it again until I am saved," and bursting out in tears, he added: "for I cannot trust myself a moment alone. I might do the same thing again; and while now I am speaking to you this horrible appetite for strong drink is coming upon me again. O Lord, save me! O Lord, save me now!"

When he thus cried, the unhappy man fell on his face and prayed God in pitiful tones to save him, right now. We all prayed with him, and I saw the dear man rising to his feet, full of hope and fear, and proclaiming the Lord to be his Saviour. He became a member of our little band.

There was the old man Watson: he kept a wretched haunt for thieves and gamblers. I visited him one evening, but when I stepped in at the front door everybody disappeared into the back part of the house. Watson knew me, and often tried to baffle my attempts to pray at his house; but at last gave it up and tried another game. He turned friendly, and even came to the meetings; but when I came to his house he managed to hide the occupants, and only three or four men would remain in the room; but he would take down the lamp from the dirty wall, and hold it while I read to the men, and then would run to the front door and shut it during prayer. Now, I could soon see through it all. Watson thought, "Now he won't be so hard on me, and ask me so much about my soul, and trouble me to give up this business. I'll just be friendly and obliging, and even tell him that I'll try to seek the Lord." But that night I had "slipped up" on him, and had seen the men disappear. I just took the old man aside, and said: "Now, Watson, it's no use your playing the hypocrite any longer. I tell you you are nearer hell to-night than you ever were in all your life; you are trying a trick on me, and the devil has been your schoolmaster. You know you are cheating yourself, and nobody else. Poor fellow! you're badly off. I pity you. I wish you would just come to Jesus to-night. You know how the Lord saved me. I've been worse than you, but Jesus took pity and saved me all over. Now, do you think I'd be wasting time with a rascal like you, if Jesus had n't picked me up, and made a new man of me? I know you think me to be just what I say I am, and now you are trying to 'smooth me over,' so that you can go on with your dirty business. Come, now, old man, and we'll pray together; but get me those men you're hiding from me. If you don't I'll turn this house upside down, and you know very well you have not got a corner in this house that I don't know. I'll find them, if you don't."

The wretched man took my hand, and said: "I know I am a bad man. Yes, I'm a bad man. I wish I could be better; but what can I do?"—"Do like I did, seek the Lord Jesus, the Saviour; confess your sins, and believe in His name. If you will quit your hypocrisy, and be in earnest about it, you'll find an earnest Saviour, who will save you in a moment."

Hunting Souls.

Then leaving Watson, I went out into the back yard, and hauled my audience out of every corner and every room, striking matches as I went on, and calling on them to come out. "I know you are here, and you need n't hide." I told them: "I love every one of you, and want you to be as happy as I am. Just see what cowards the devil makes of you! The light of a match scares you to death, and you feel ashamed when you think of it. Now, come, let's have a meeting." Sometimes, in other places, they did the same thing, and in that way I would often hunt up eight or ten men, and the meeting would always be a wonderful blessing. Oh, praise the Lord! how these difficulties and hardships made the word clear and blessed to myself and them! I could now read human nature, as I never could before. My faith in God became simpler, more childlike, and peaceful. There was no power on earth nor in hell that could stop the progress of the Lord's work in those dens of wickedness. Though often in imminent danger, God — the blessed Holy Ghost — a personal Holy Ghost — seemed so real in His abiding presence, that I was perfectly conscious of His walking in me, and living in me. The supernatural agency ever present in protecting me, had become more real to me than I can express with the words of faith. But it seemed visible to my eyes, and tangible to the grasp of my hand. Holding my Bible seemed to me as taking hold of the sword, and in it I possessed the Holy Ghost. I shall never be able to fathom all I know and feel, or to express it in my poor language; but I think the language of heaven will bring it all out, and relieve me from the weight that I feel hanging to my tongue now, without being able to shake it off; and I believe "the mists will roll away," that now cloud my poor brain. The *twilight* of the resurrection morn will break into a fair and ever-sunny day. No more "supposing Him to be," we understand and give Him all the glory. Yet it is but in part we know, and "Who is Christ?" in heaven's light appears in fullest meaning. We will and shall be able to tell it all in glory. The angels cannot tell it, but the blood-washed can, quite well. Amen. Praise the Lord, O my soul, for ever and ever!

A Terrible Death.

A few days after this talk with Watson, I was called out, after an evening meeting. Some men came up and asked me to go with them to Watson's place — something awful had happened. It was only about fifty yards from the meeting-room, and I soon reached the place. I found a great many people crowded about the door, and looking rather strange. "What is the matter?" I inquired of the men. "Go in and see, sir." I made my way through the crowd, and in the dark and filthy-looking room where he had often heard me speak and pray, there lay Watson, stretched on a board upon two chairs — a corpse! He was dead! I stood there for a few moments, and could not say a word. One of the men then said: "You see, Mr. Krauser, they've had a big time here to-night. They had dancing, and Watson got awfully drunk, and while he was dancing and jumping about, he all of a sudden fell down. We thought he had only fallen down because he was so drunk; but when we went to help him up, we saw that he was dead." That was the terrible end of the rum-seller. I turned and gave my message to the bystanders. The moment was an awful one. There lay the victim of rum. Few men heard the Gospel as this man had heard it! It had been a savor unto death to him. I said: "Be not deceived. God is not mocked — what a man soweth that shall he also reap. Awful judgment! My God, save this people! Now you want me to bury this man; yes, that is the way you do. When one dies you send for the clergyman to bury your dead, — that is the way you treat your loving Saviour. But funeral sermons won't save you. You know how Watson used to live, and you know how he died, and so shall every one die who will not come to God. It will come upon you like a thief in the night, in an hour when you think not. Be ye therefore ready. If you will all come to the funeral, and bring your friends with you, I will bury this man and preach to you in the chapel of the cemetery."

When I had said this, and appointed the hour, I left them, and went away deeply impressed with what I had seen and heard this night. While others were being saved, this man sank into a drunkard's grave. This case was similar to one sometime ago in a German family. Two daughters of this family had joined the German Methodist Church which I had organized in this city. The mother, who was extremely worldly and very fond of dancing, had been exhorted by her children to give up the world. This was on Saturday, and they had asked her to come with them to church to-morrow. But the mother said no, she would never come to church, nor could she believe in the existence of God. The poor children were frightened at what the mother said, and with tears begged her to recant what she had just uttered; but she would not do it. Then they begged her to give up a party which she was to attend that night, and stay with the children, for they feared to let her go after she had said that she did not believe in God. But she said: "I will go, and if it is for the last time, I shall have a dance." That unhappy mother was carried to her home, a corpse, early on Sunday morning. She had fainted, apparently, while dancing. Friends laid her on the sofa; but the woman never arose. She had died of heart disease, — not, however, without a warning.

CHAPTER XI.

TIMES OF SPECIAL VISITATION.

No wonder people began to consider the question of salvation, and the spirit of inquiry at this time was something wonderful. On shore, and in the bay, the soul-saving work was going on. The Holy Spirit smote the hearts of the people everywhere, and daily precious souls were brought to Jesus. On one ship in the bay — the *Seneca* — five men were converted to God; on another, the *Stormy Petrel*, the entire ship's company, from the chief officer down to the last man on board, were converted, and three of the number found holiness before the ship left for England. On board a third ship, the fire spread, and one of the men tried to run away from God. When he saw me coming down to the forecastle, he hid himself, but I was looking for him. I knew every place and corner in the ship, and I started for the chain-locker — a place where chains and ropes were kept. It had only a small door to it, just large enough for a man to crawl through. I opened it and struck a match; but I could not see anything. He could not be anywhere else, as I had looked carefully about me on the outside. So I crawled in on all fours, shut the door behind me, and lighted several matches, and crawled into every nook and corner. At last I discovered my man, — he had pulled a lot of ropes over his head, but there he was. My matches had given out, and I said: "Ah, there you are! just stay where you are — we'll have it out right there." So I crawled up to him in the dark, and began to pray with him there. He was deeply convicted for sin, and he knew his hour had come when he must settle the question with God. I was glad that I had found him, for I soon heard him weep there in the dark, and he finally prayed for himself. We then left this place together, and the young man looked like a new man. He could praise God indeed, for deliverance from the power of darkness. His soul had been turned to the light.

The funeral service of Watson was a wonderful meeting. Everybody in the chapel was on their knees, and I believe this place had never witnessed such a meeting before. At the close I gave them another invitation to the mission-room, and most of those present at the funeral promptly responded, and the evening was remarkable.

An Aged Drunkard Converted.

A man who had been a drunkard for twenty years, prayed for pardon, and another whom drink had brought to the verge of the grave, prayed earnestly that God might save him from his sins. Both men were converted to God. The one became a faithful worker as a member of our band, and God used him wonderfully among his friends. The other man died three days afterward, in his room. The night previous he had been at the meeting in the room where God converted him. He was then so weak that he could hardly stand on his feet, and with a trembling voice he gave his testimony for Christ, and said that God had kept him faithful since the moment he had found peace; and although he knew that when he gave up drink it would kill him, as he had gone too far already, yet he would not touch a drop to steady his nerves. He said he knew he had not long to live, but he desired only one thing — to die in faith; and then he asked us to pray for him. His speech seemed peculiarly impressive, as he stood there; his long snowy hair, that trembling, earnest voice, and his beaming face. No one thought that this was his last testimony for Jesus on earth. We should see his face no more. He was found dead in his bed the next morning. He had gone to heaven to see his Saviour, whom he had found; but alas! so late.

I was much grieved to find that two men, who had professed conversion some time ago, had gone back to the world, — the one to drink; but the other in a moment of severe temptation yielded and stole the sum of eighty dollars from a Christian brother with whom he occupied a room. Oh, how bitter that was! I wept before the Lord, and wondered why this was permitted to befall me. I could tell no one my griefs, for who could understand me? It was a terrible blow. A few days later I received a letter from the man, telling me about his terrible struggle, and how at last he yielded. He had taken the money and spent it all in these few nights, and then he closed this sad letter with — "I am lost." The brother who had lost the money in this way, bore the loss in wonderful submission to the Lord. He had worked hard for it, and since the Lord had converted him had been able to save this amount. He was the same man who, a few months ago, had received the Saviour and was taken to the hospital the following day. He was now one of the noblest workers in our fellowship band.

Organization of a Good Templars' Lodge.

My Sunday meetings in saloon No. 1 and No. 2, had now for some time been discontinued, on account of the work increasing in the mission-room; but the places had been visited the same as the others; but now I made a call on Mr. B., in No. 1, and asked him to attend a temperance meeting, to be held to-morrow night. He promised to be there. Invitations were given to as many as we could seat, and the meeting night drew near. A good many persons were in attendance, especially those residing in the city — Americans, English, Swedes, and Germans. After delivering my lecture, a table was brought to the platform and an invitation was given to step forward to sign the temperance pledge. The first man that left the ranks of the enemy was Mr. B., rum-seller No. 1. We shook hands, and he said, honestly: "I've enough of this now — I quit it to-night, God helping me." He gave up his saloon, and kept only boarders; but business was very dull. He had lost many customers, but he was not discouraged. The following night I organized a Lodge of Good Templars, and all those who had signed the pledge, and others, were present. Fifty-one members were received into the order the first evening, and soon we numbered one hundred and fifty. The principal point in the work had been gained. These men were drawn from the dens of vice, and many had been converted, and others became teetotalers — working in the cause of temperance. The result was that six of the rum-sellers had to close their saloons, and look for other employment.

A Sailors' Home Called into Being.

I then called upon some of my ministerial brethren and told them the time had come when something must be done for the seamen coming to this port. There was no home for them here — they had no place where they were well-treated and cared for — and I asked them to assist in raising the necessary funds. Dr. T., of Valparaiso, who has been working here for the last forty years, took a lively interest in this new plan, and influenced some of the members of his church to give money. Some merchants also helped, and several thousand dollars were raised to buy the necessary furniture. The house was soon found, and rented. It was an old hotel, containing fifty-four rooms.

An Ex-Rumseller Becomes the Administrator of the Sailors' Home.

Now, the proper man for the home was found in my friend and reformed rumseller No. 1. "God bless you!" I said to Mr. B., as I told him I wanted him for the Sailors' Home. He was much surprised at first; but joyfully accepted. After the first three months, the house was self-supporting. It paid the house-rent of $150 per month, the salary of the administrator, the wages of all the servants, and all the expenses to run the institution. Meetings were established in the house for the seamen, and I placed the first books into the library, and went about begging books for the Home wherever I could, and printed the labels on my handpress to paste on the books. And nobly did the friends assist me in starting this Seamen's Home. The *Record*, the organ of an English Church of this place, said, in a report some time after: "And Rev. Von Barchwitz-Krauser assisted in starting the Seamen's Home." Now, I wonder whether the church members or the merchants wanted the glory of this work, or whether it would be better to give it to God alone. It would have been better to say nothing, if they could not come out squarely and say: "All glory be to God for our Sailors' Home!" How many persons are there in the world that are just proud enough to give some money and then expect to be praised for it, and think that it is all the work required of them. Such will not bend a finger to bring it about; but when the Lord has done it, some "graciously" give, and say: "Now, I did it!" They have hired the Lord to do it for them. God save us from all pride and vain-glory, through the truth! The word of God is sharper than any two-edged sword, — cutting, piercing, and dividing asunder to the bones and marrow; and we might as well face the truth while yet on earth, and stand the "trimming," and we shall all be better prepared to bring forth fruit, and thus glorify God, who will not give His glory to another. When men do attempt to get glory to themselves, they are often put to shame immediately. Proud boasters become cowards, and must flee.

I had visited a brothel, together with a brother whom his shipmates formerly called the "ship's devil." We found six young men there, apprentices from some of the sailing-vessels in the harbor. After shaking hands all around, I sat down to read the word to them, and then exhorted them to come to Jesus. One of the men began to swear at me and use profane language. I only replied: "We will now talk with God, and pray." The young man now jumped up, and angrily confronting me, said: "If you attempt to pray here, I'll stand on my head, sir."—"All right, my boy; you stand on your head, and I will pray. Let us see who can hold out longest." Without saying more, we all knelt in prayer. While praying there was great quietness in the room, only once there was a rustling behind me, and some one opening a door, and closing it with a bang. God had blessed us in praying, and I called also on the brother to pray, who did so. When we arose, I turned about, and said: "Where is the man that would stand on his head?"—"He ran away, sir, when you had knelt down to pray." Ah, yes, poor fellows, cannot bear the presence of God when brought in contact with Him in the house of prayer. Their glorying in their own strength, and vain boasting, is put to shame.

Opinions of some Ship-Masters.

Some five masters of ships told me one day: "Now, Mr. Krauser, it is no use doing anything for a sailor, — the best treatment is a belaying-pin across the head, and a few good kicks."—"Now, friends," I said, "you are not alone in this; you've got one who is quite in sympathy with you on this point, and that is your master, the devil; but you are not the men to encourage me in my work, and so I trust the Lord and go right ahead. Satan wants no better thing to accomplish his designs, than men like you; but, remember, Jesus reigneth, and His has had the victory over many a poor, down-trodden sailor, and He will be victor always."

The leader in this conversation — an American captain — a few days after was taken to the hospital. He had lost his reason. When he got a little better, they sent him home, where he died soon after. It seems hard, but God does not need such men to live on the earth; but they can be saved, and God can use them. O that man might cease to merely "exist," but *live!*

A poor sailor, who had often attended our meetings, instead of coming to God and accepting the invitation of Jesus, got worse and worse. When he attended the meeting the other night, it was to be the last night that we could pray with him. He left the room, and said: " It's no use, I won't be a Christian," and he went and made himself drunk — so much so, that in the night, walking along the water's edge, on the landing-pier, he fell over, and before he could be taken up out of the water, he was drowned. What shall I say to these things? They are awful records. O that God would impress us solemnly to live as in the sight of eternity, and with holy and pure lives, that we might be princes, — kings and priests unto God; and as such, to have power with God and with men, and be thoroughly furnished unto all good works, that we might by all means save some — that we might go into the highways and search the hedges, and compel them to hear the Gospel. Thank God! there are ways to compel sinners to hear the Gospel.

A German, who kept a drinking-place and brothel, forbade me emphatically to come into his house; but in front of his door, on the street, he had no right over me, and so we had some meetings there.

A Street-Meeting in Front of a Brothel.

One day, however, he managed to set some young men on the track, to disturb us, and, if possible, to pick a quarrel with me. Most of the rumsellers had given up this work in despair, for I would never quarrel; but this German was a hard case. However, as in this case, he did not try it himself, but always sent some poor, unsuspecting sailors, to put their fingers into the fire for him. A few glasses of beer or whiskey, and now for "the fun." They came out and began their manœuvres. I stopped talking, of course, and after waiting a few moments, said: "Now, as soon as you are through with what you have to say, I'll go on." For a minute or two they looked at me, and I had just taken up my subject, when one of the party stepped in front of me, and said: "Now, here, stop that nonsense. You needn't preach to us about these stories, we don't believe you, anyway." But now matters looked different, — several men in the crowd raised their voices in my defence, and as the young man made no signs te retreat, the men walked up and were about to give the fellow a sound thrashing. I interposed at once, and the enemy got out of sight in double quick. The audience had doubled in number by this time, and I went on preaching to them, and then marched them off to the mission-room. Some followed, and some did not; but those who did were richly blesssed, and so as to leave a hope that I shall meet a few in heaven; and I pray God that sooner or later, all who heard the word preached by his humble servant, in simple faith, in these parts of God's vineyard, in some way may be brought to Christ.

It was remarkable in what way and manner the enemy of mankind sometimes would try to place hindrances in the way of the work. After a Sabbath's service in the harbor, on the Monday following, a captain came to me on the street, in great anger, and said: "Mr. Krauser, I have sworn to hinder your work in the bay in every possible way I can. If I can do it, you shall not have a ship for service while I am here in the harbor. Yesterday, while you were preaching on the main deck, a lot of sailors from other ships remained in the forecastle and had bottles of whiskey with them, and they, with a few of the men belonging to the ship, got drunk, and the captain got in great trouble with the men. Now your work must be stopped." Shaking his fist, he left me.

A Bit of Advice.

Next day I visited that captain on board of his ship, and had a good long talk with him. I told him that the officers of the ship were to be blamed if there was any blame to it, and not the preaching of the Gospel; "but if you godless captains can throw dirt on Christ, and His work, you are only too ready to do it. Do n't you think one of the officers might stand at the head of the gangway and see to it that every visitor takes his seat where such has been provided for him?"—"Yes, yes, you 're right. I think that 's a good idea."—"Now, are you not ashamed of your conduct yesterday?"—"Ah, now you are pushing me too close, sir."—"No, I do n't; you were one of that crowd yesterday who cried out some years ago: 'Away with Him! away with Him!' and rather desired a thief or a murderer, and would not that Christ should go on in His work, and bless my sailor boys. Is it not so?"—"Well," said he, "that 's rough, but never mind; you just come here next Sunday, and announce service to be held on board my ship for that day."—"Now, that is sensible enough," I said to him; "but if you don't give up your drinking and all the rest of your sins, you cannot save your soul; and I hope that you will begin this day to pray to God for Christ's sake to forgive you." The poor man could not see his way clear to do that, "at once," but when I left him he had received more light on the subject of Christian religion than he ever had before, and I do hope the dear Saviour will lead the captain to repentance. Thus the devices of the enemy are frustrated, and the blessed Redeemer is glorified. Truly, also, God taketh the wise in their own craftiness, and causes His children to praise Him. I do pray God that the design in writing these experiences in the work, may be accomplished, and lead sinners to seek their God, and see how terribly the enemy deceives poor blind sinners; and, secondly, bless Christians in reading this, in such a way that they may go out to work for God in winning souls for Jesus, and laugh at impossibilities, and know that perfect love casteth out all fear.

How I Paid a Debt.

How wonderfully God will provide us with things we need, can be seen by the following experience, which I desire to tell to the glory of God.

For a considerable time I had been much depressed in my heart, because of the debt of $180, we still owed for our furniture. Eight months had passed since the purchase, but our income supplied only the running expenses. I at once prayed to God to send the money to pay that debt, *now*. I told my wife, and we prayed together. The following day the burden of that debt increased, and I said to wife: "You pray here in the dining-room, while I pray up stairs: and we will both pray that the Lord may send us the money at once." Now, while praying, I felt something was giving way, and I obtained the promise, "When you pray, believe that you receive it, and ye shall have it." I claimed the amount. The burden left me immediately, and I arose with great peace in my soul. Going down stairs my dear wife came to meet me, and her face looked so bright when she said, "The Lord has heard us, and I can rest now: He will give it to us." She had received the same blessing while I prayed up stairs. In the afternoon, a Christian brother, but poor in worldly possessions, who had received the blessing of a clean heart in one of my meetings, called on me. I was glad to see him, and he said: "Brother, we have been much exercised on your account since yesterday. We felt to pray much for you, and I have come over to see what is really the matter here at your home." I felt so happy and peaceful in my heart, that I did not think about our last two days' experience, and did not for a moment think the brother alluded to it, as he could not possibly know anything about our wants. So I just told him I was glad he prayed for us, and that I felt much disposed to praise the Lord all day long, and added: "If, at any time, God has blessed me and my wife, it is surely now," and that I did not see that anything else was the matter. The brother seemed glad to hear this, and said that he had been impressed by the Spirit to come over and see me, and as everything was all right, he started to go back home, after we had spoken about some other things. I went with him to the door. Then he took my hand, and looking at me, said: "Now, brother, are you sure there is nothing you want?" I did not understand what he meant, and I told him so. He then said in an undertone: "Bro. K., I know you have not been able to pay for your furniture yet; you did not know that I was acquainted with the fact, and when yesterday, during family prayers, we prayed for you, and again this morning, we were much concerned about you, and I do n't know how it came, but I thought about that debt. I cannot help you, dear brother, you know that; but we can help you pray for the money." While the brother was talking thus I could hold back no longer. I had listened with amazement to what he said, and now I told him my experience, and how, for the last two days, we had prayed to God for that very same thing. The brother was overjoyed to hear what he did, and grasping my hand, said: "Surely God is sending you the money: I will go on praying until you do get it." Now that was remarkable, and as I sat down with my wife, we talked about this, and wondered what would come next. We felt as if at any moment some one might step into the room and give us the money. But evening came and nothing had arrived yet. Our faith was severely tried — it was quite certain the money was to come somehow that night. Both I and my wife had never felt so trustful and resting upon God as in this particular case, and there was no wavering experienced. We had just finished our supper, when the bell rang. I opened the door and admited the brother who had called on me in the afternoon, accompanied by his wife. We welcomed them heartily and invited them in. We had conversed only a few minutes, when the brother took a letter from his pocket and handed it to me; and I, thanking him, put it into my pocket, to read it after the visitors should have retired. But he said: "Not so, I want you to read it now, and give me an answer." I saw both he and his wife smiling, so I opened the letter, and there was nothing written in it; but I held in my trembling hand two one-hundred dollar bills. I could not speak, but I wept. The joy was too much for me. I arose and embracing the brother, I wept on his neck, while the two sisters did the same. Then I pressed my wife to my heart, and tenderly kissing her, I said: "God is good." — "Yes," was all she could whisper. It was a great blessing to us, and a scene which angels love to behold. When we had recovered somewhat, I wanted to know all about it — how the Lord had provided that money, for I knew that this poor man did not possess that amount to give away. He said: "It is very simple. Soon after I left you in the afternoon, I had some business down town. A gentleman had told me to come to his office and get a key to his house, which I was to clean up, and do some painting. After I had made my arrangement with him, he said: "Mr. W., you are a friend of Mr. K.?"—"Yes, sir." — "You know how he is getting along?"—"Yes, he is getting along well — the Lord is blessing him in his work." — "Well, that is not what I mean. I know that: but how is he getting along financially?"—"Oh, I guess pretty well." — "Do you know whether he is in need just now?"—"Yes, I believe he is just now in a little pinch." — "Well, I thought so. Now, Mr. W., do me the favor to hand to Mr. K. this envelope. I had it ready to send before you came in, but as you live near by, just run over. I am glad to have heard what you said." Bro. W. continued and said: "I myself did not know how much there was in that envelope; I had no idea; but I trusted the Lord would make it all right." Now, could we not all see the hand of God so plain in this whole matter from beginning to end? How did God use just these two men, and in particular this poor man, to be the messenger to bring the letter to our house! What a blessing it proved to be to both! Oh, how good and kind is our Heavenly Father! We had a regular good old-fashioned Methodist class-meeting before we separated, telling what God had done for us in the past. There was no need to say: "Lord, increase our faith." Walking in the light, we simply would believe — take God at His word. We had received above that which we had asked. Praise His name!

TOBACCO EXPERIENCES.

In a meeting on board ship, I gave my experience in tobacco. At the close a captain present related the following: "Tobacco, for a long time, held me a prisoner, as it does most sailors, until one day the light came to me that it was rather a foolish way of spending money, and that this money belonged to the Lord, and that I had no right to consume it on such an appetite as that. So I laid tobacco aside from a sense of duty. I was tempted severely, and I thought, 'I am able to fight against it,' and I rather took pride in the thought that I could. One morning, however, I caught myself stuffing a pipe, and never found it out until I struck a match to light it. I felt ashamed. I laid it aside and said: 'I'll never touch it again!' Soon after I was called to take my ship to Smyrna, and run against two fine clipper-ships. The owners of the ships had set out a ten-pound note for the one who should reach the port first. You cannot imagine how I was tempted on tobacco during that voyage, as for hours I walked the deck, watching the wind and weather, in order to take every possible advantage. I felt a burning desire to smoke — to be occupied with something. But now comes the fight and the victory. The devil told me, 'You must get your pipe.' I ran down into my cabin, and falling down upon my knees, prayed God to cleanse my heart from this desire for the filthy stuff. It then occurred to me that I had not been to God with it before. I prayed now for God to save me, and then and there I was delivered. My work on deck was now much easier, and my undivided attention was given to the sailing. I did not have that feeling of ease and carelessness that one experiences in smoking. My ship was in Smyrna two days before the two other vessels." Another captain said: " One day, walking on deck, I was clearly convicted about my smoking. I took the short pipe out of my mouth, and looking at it, I clenched my fist and just said: 'What! you dirty little black pipe, you were trying to get me under, and make me your slave! Never!' and with that I suited the action to the word, and threw pipe and tobacco overboard, and then, thanked God for deliverance, and like my friend, Captain Parnell, I have never been troubled with a desire since."

Prayer on a Jib-Boom.

The Lord converted three of the seamen on board of the ship *Rose of Devon*. Another had sat down on the jib-boom, hoping to be out of reach. I went after him, and holding on to the ropes, I prayed with him there.

That afternoon I visited the hospital, and saw a sick man. He sat near the window, between two beds. After conversing with him for a time, I asked him whether I should pray with him. He replied that I might save myself the trouble. I said it was not any trouble, and I knelt down and prayed. The poor man arose from his seat, and stepping over my head, went away; but I prayed on. The man went as far as the door, then he stopped and watched me. When I came towards him he went away. David says: "Thou alone makest me to dwell in safety." Those who turn away from God are not safe. Whether sick or well, can we lie down and sleep in peace outside of God? What an opportunity the sick have to commune with their own hearts (Ps. iv.)! Not always, however. Many have waited, and put off the day of salvation.

In the Grip of Death.

I was called to the Sailors' Home, and led into a room where a dying man lay on his bed. He had called for me. He made signs with his hand that I should sit down near him. To my astonishment he began to talk about worldly things, and seemed to be eagerly expecting that I should tell him that he would get better, while death was actually fastened on his face, and the doctor had told him to prepare for death. He could not believe it. The poor, unhappy man — I pitied him intensely; and I began to point out Christ to him. To my great astonishment he said: "Please don't speak to me of that. I can't bear to hear that name." I held his hand, and looking at him, said: "My dear friend, how can you speak like that, with no prospect of life before you? Do think of making your peace with God." With an effort the man raised himself in the bed, and those ghastly eyes were fixed upon me, and in an angry tone he said: "Do leave the room. I tell you I don't want to hear of that name." I rose from my chair, and was just about speaking again, when, with a thundering voice, he exclaimed: "Leave the room! leave the room! or I will throw this chair at you! I will not die! Go, leave the room!" — "God have mercy on you!" I said, and then, with a sad heart, left the room. In the morning of the following day, I was called to the Seamen's Home again, to make arrangements for the burial of the man. He had passed away his life in sin, and they told me he died miserably, though conscious to the last.

In the midst of these dark scenes in the work, there

came days when the heart was made glad. I visited a ship in the harbor and preached on board, one Sabbath, and in the afternoon held an extra meeting in the forecastle, with the men, for I had noticed during the morning service that some were convicted of sin by the Spirit. There was a wonderful feeling manifested among them, and the Lord gave me one soul. Then the men told me how easy it was to become a better man on board of their ship in comparison to other ships, and it was touching how they spoke of the captain's wife. They said: "She will often talk to us about our souls, and give us tracts and good books, and then she will make us bring our clothes and she will patch them for us, and make us keep them in good order." How blessed is such a testimony from the sailors on board a ship, and it tells me what a blessed influence a Christian captain, or a Christain wife of a captain, may exercise on a ship. They closed their beautiful story in saying: "Why, she is like a mother to us!" God bless that dear woman, on board of the *Formosa!*

On board of the *Beechwood* we had blessed meetings during the week, and on the Sabbath.

Deciding for Christ on the Gangway.

God had converted some of the men, and just before the ship left her moorings to sail for England, I saw her off, and on the gangway the chief officer gave his heart to Jesus, and taking hold of my hand, said: "Bro. K., by the grace of God I will meet you in heaven!" That was a glorious parting, and I felt the Lord had sent me on board to receive this mate's testimony. The ship hove up her anchors, and was taken outside the bay and fastened to a buoy, to await a favorable breeze, and before it came the crew had an opportunity to prove in a degree their sincerity, and the effect of the word of God upon their hearts, in a remarkable way. Coming on shore I went to the office of a merchant who was the treasurer of the Seamen's Society, in order to give him $22, which some parties had given me for the work. Somehow I had lost that that money. I felt sorry, but what could I do? When I discovered the loss, I said with all my heart, "Praise the Lord!" and taking out of my pocket-book another $22, went and paid it, telling the treasurer that I had just lost the original bills. I left the store and ran up to my house to get dinner. When I told my good wife about the money lost, she told me that perhaps I was careless in not putting it with the money I carried in the pocket-book; but it was not that exactly, I had only in haste taken out my note-book, instead of the pocket bank note-book, and had lost it with the money. I felt somehow that I could pray for the finding of the money, and knowing also that we could not well suffer the loss of $22, we placed it in humble prayer before the Lord.

About two in the afternoon, I told my wife I would go down town the same road that I had taken in the morning, feeling as though I would find the money. She looked doubtful, and I said: "Now, be praying and believing while I go and look." Following the road toward the harbor I looked about me every step almost, but nothing could be seen, and my faith was tried, and I said to myself: "Praise the Lord! I will have it yet." Just then some one called my name. I looked up and saw Capt. P., of the *Beechwood*, running towards me in great haste, and pressing a closed envelope into my hand, said: "This is from the crew. You know I heard you lost $22. Mr. H. told me so when I went to get my papers for the ship. I went on board and dropped the remark, and the chief officer heard it, so he went back to the men, and they made a list, and in five minutes the whole amount was subscribed. Then they begged me to go on shore and deposit the money with some one, as I did not expect to meet you." I had hardly time to thank the captain. He said a hasty good-by, and "in half an hour we'll be off," jumped into his boat, and away he went. God made me find the money. Amen! Praise the Lord! There are millions of people who should invest money in the Lord's work; but what do they rather use it for? To consume it upon their own desire — lust. When will men begin to count the returns for their hard-earned, and so easy-spent, money? To lay up never-failing treasures in heaven is little thought of on this line; but there will be a weighing in the balance some day. What do men give to gain money? Reputation and honor, yea, their strength and life-blood. How many respectable thieves and robbers have we about us, and in our home circles. When some have taken the first step they still tremble, but the second step they sat down quite easy. But thanks be to God! some are being rescued from this dreadful hell.

BE SURE YOUR SIN WILL FIND YOU OUT.

A young man attended my meetings, and one night he followed me nearly to my house, and I did not know it. Just about to turn the corner of a street, where there stood a lamp-post, lighting the road up to my house on a hill, he touched me on the shoulder, and said, "Excuse me, Mr. Krauser, but I must speak with you." I had turned about and taken his hand, and waited for him to say on; but the poor fellow would not say a word. He trembled as he looked to the ground, and then the tears began to flow. I let him take his time, feeling deeply for him as he stood there. "Tell me all, my dear friend; if you had no confidence, you would not have followed me so far." He then began as follows: "I had the contract with a glazier to make the windows of a large building belonging to the government, and when the work was finished he came to me and said: 'Now, Mr. M——, we might make a little extra on this work. You know I took this job cheaper than anyone else would, and this is the government, and they don't mind paying, if we put down on the bill a few hundred window-panes more. You know I don't make anything anyway, and if you agree I'll divide with you.' Oh, Mr. Krauser, you see I gave way! He handed in his bill, and then we divided, and now this money is in my pocket, and it burns me to my bones. Oh, I can't bear it! it troubles me so that in some way I must get rid of it; and, besides, I feel that I'm a wretched man, and lost. Oh, that God might, for Christ's sake, forgive me my sins! Oh, do pray for me, Mr. Krauser!" The unhappy man took my hand, and imploringly looked into my face. I saw he was in earnest, so I knelt down beside the lamp-post and he followed the example. There was no time to be lost, and he began to pray for himself. Yes, and God answered our united prayer on the spot. As the light of that lamp-post shone down upon us, so did the light from Calvary shine into that man's heart. The first thing he said when he rose was, "Now, by the help of God, I shall go to the man who tempted me and throw the Judas money on the counter as soon as he opens the store in the morning." I met the young man next day. He looked so bright and cheerful. "Well, M., how is it now?" "Oh, praise the Lord! I am saved and free! I gave up the money, and the man said to me that I was a fool, and I answered him, yes I was a fool, to lose my soul for the sake of money, but thank God, I have the salvation of Christ in my soul. Glory be to God for deliverance!" For the sake of the soul, let no man be ensnared by money: it is the metal of the chain that binds them in hell.

CHAPTER XII.

IN THE FIERY FURNACE WITH JESUS. — UNEXPECTED CHANGES.

UNDER such manifest blessings of God, the new year — 1883 — drew near, and during the month of January the Lord, in such a wonderful way, poured out His blessing upon the work, as we probably had not felt or seen in all the three years of the past. There was no "excitement," but a steady, certain giving way of the powers of darkness in every meeting during the week, and on the Sabbath. In the hospital work, and in the harbor, daily, souls were brought to Christ; and such a mighty inquiry prevailed, that every day, from the early morning up to late at night (sometimes 11 o'clock), I was engaged visiting the workshops on shore, and the shipping in the bay, and holding meetings in the evening, either on shore, at the mission-room, or on board ship among the sailors in the forecastle; as also in the rum-shops in the "Maintop." At one of the meetings at the room, eleven members of our band stepped into the blessing of entire sanctification, and three hardened sinners were converted to God. Visiting two ships ready to leave the port, I spoke to the crew once more, and several received Christ before I left the ship. One man, who had kept from giving himself up entirely, for cleansing, stepped out on the promise, "I will keep him in perfect peace whose mind is stayed on Me, because he trusteth in Me,"— by faith, — perfect peace — a stayed mind. He understood me perfectly, and with a beaming face he said: "Glory to God! He cleanseth me now!" His trouble had been concerning evil thoughts; hence this text from Isaiah was blessed to him. He could not distinguish between "evil thoughts" and "thoughts of evil," and the enemy had troubled him much and long about it, until he almost despaired of ever getting rid of evil thoughts, as he expressed himself.

A tidal wave of salvation had swept over us for three years, and we had not got over it yet. My heart was filled with praises toward God, for truly wonderful works were done through the name of the Lord Jesus Christ, and all the glory belongs to God.

Taking leave of the men on a ship, one followed me on deck and there spoke to me. He could not go out to sea without Jesus, and Jesus did not let him go without, for, up on deck, under the "mizzen," He saved the dear boy, and with his eyes beaming for gladness, he ran to his work. While speaking to the men on another ship in the evening, just before returning on shore to open the mission-room, I dropped the remark, "You cannot be on square accounts with God, and not know it."

A sailor arose and exclaimed, " Praise God, I see it all now! yes, glory to God! I know this moment the question is settled, I am the Lord's, and Jesus saves me this moment."

The Gospel for the Natives.

On shore the Lord had converted a native, who daily went about the city selling Bibles and Testaments to his countrymen, and he was wonderfully successful in his sales. Everywhere, in the harbor especially, men were found grouping together along the landing-stages, and reading God's word, and early in the morning, at 6 o'clock, twice every week, I took position there and distributed reading matter to the natives. Oftentimes I was surrounded by hundreds, and it was pleasing to see how eagerly they would devour the tracts with their eyes, and then read to those who could not. Policemen and custom-house officers alike were anxious to receive tracts, and would force their way to me, and they generally succeeded better than any one else, as their official robe was respected. I should have often been over-run by the crowd, and then I took my stand close to the water's edge. Now I was safe, for they took good care not to push me over into the water, and under God I could trust them perfectly; but, besides, I knew every one loved to see me. Then the boats were remembered, which by this time had collected in great numbers. Jumping into one of them, I began to distribute. These days were feast-days in the harbor.

Shadows of the Valley.

But now came upon me the greatest trial of my life. In the midst of such work, I must cease to work; yea, more than that, leave this place, which by this time had become so dear to me. When I was asked once by the oldest missionary on the coast — Dr. Trumbull — how long I expected to remain in the country, my answer was, "A life-time." The good Dr. liked that; he thought this to be the only way to do lasting good, and I agreed with him in this. And yet I must go. My poor wife had been failing in health for nearly two years. It had become an object of daily prayer; but she got worse and worse. To relieve her in her housework, the Lord sent us sufficient means to hire two servants, — one for the housework and the other for our children, — the Lord having blessed us with two dear little boys. But all this seemed to be of no effect. Three trips to the South did not prove to be of much benefit. On the contrary, every time she returned to Valparaiso her health was declining. However, the thought that we would ever be compelled to leave the work on this account, for a change of climate, never entered our mind, until at last one of the best physicians, who attended my wife, insisted on our going to

Europe. Heart disease, and the symptoms of consumption, had made their appearance in an appalling manner. Oh, how I was tried! I had been so taken up with the work that the fact became a trial to me, supposing that I had not heeded the entreaties of my dear wife long before, although I knew she had suffered so much for some time. In this hour of my greatest trial, oh, how I felt the sustaining power of my blessed Jesus! While writing down these lines, tears fill my eyes,—tears of thankfulness and gratitude towards the Mighty to save. The enemy of my soul tried hard to shake my faith, and most severely thrust those things at me, which, under such circumstances, in relation to family affairs, are used by him. Days of fasting and prayer followed. Brethren and sisters were consulted, and from some came opposition to my leaving; others, again, said I must go. My physical strength threatened to give way, being crowded on every hand; but deliverance did come, and I expected it, praise the Lord!

A Struggle for Light.

Bro. Collyer, from Iquique, who supplied the pulpit of the Union church for a time, came to me late one evening. My wife had retired with the children, and I lay on the floor in the parlor, praying. When I admitted him, he fell on my neck, and we kissed each other. We remained in each other's embrace for some minutes;

neither one of us could speak a word. He then led me to the sofa, and now came the deliverance. Bro. Collyer talked to me, and we prayed together. He stayed with me until after twelve o'clock. I think it was past one when he left. But what transpired during these hours, I cannot describe. I want to be spared to relate the bitter, — be spared to relate the sweet, that put out the bitter. It is so glorious, the remembrance of that hour! The tremendous weight that had almost crushed me, had rolled away. Bro. Collyer was sick — the same trouble as my darling wife, except the heart disease; and he thought that sometime he should leave. Yes, only too soon he left! The result of that night's meeting, was our decision to go on a trip to Europe, and thence return to the United States.

On Feb. 6, I installed the officers of my Good Templars' Lodge for the last quarter. The work among them is a blessing to the community. Clergymen of other denominations had taken interest in the temperance work, and helped much to spread the cause.

My German Methodist Church.

I had organized my German Methodist Church with twenty-four members. The temperance work and the direct religious work had been done in halls not belonging to us. Ground and buildings being very high, we could not gain property, and had not been able to so keep the people together, as to justify an organization among the English-speaking people of the community; in fact, under the circumstances, I encouraged them to join other churches, for they must needs have a home.

The unpleasant task of packing trunks began now, and the selling of furniture. I found that we had, during the three years, accumulated property to the amount of $600 in Chili paper; however, this left us just with our personal effects. I received $100 as a present from a clergyman, and this enabled us to buy a second-class ticket to Liverpool. We had only seven pounds sterling left, but we were willing to trust God for the future, as we had done in the past. A long sea-voyage would be necessary for my wife, and I used this opportunity to visit Germany after an absence from the "Fatherland" of thirteen years, and, if it pleased God, to preach there.

We had the great joy of entertaining Dr. Taylor at our house. He had come to South America a short time ago, and when he found the necessity of my leaving Valparaiso, he came down to arrange to put in another man in the work; but now it was found that the merchants and others who had given money towards the support of the mission, had agreed with the Union Church committee not to receive any of Taylor's men, but make the work one of their own, as they considered now that it virtually had belonged to them all the while; because, being largely members of that church, they had been giving to the Seamen's Mission of their money. Now a change being necessary, they thought the time had come to take it into their own hands; which they voted upon, and gave Mr. Taylor to understand it; however, not directly. He was permitted to find it out for himself. To God belongs the glory of the past, and the glory of the future work, whoever is to carry it on.

This was another trial before I left. The work was left without a man to do the work. I had held, during the three years in Valparaiso, from Jan. 2, 1880, up to Feb. 19, 1883, 1,415 meetings. My last meeting in the harbor, Feb. 18, was on board the *Arequipa*, in the forenoon, and in the afternoon preaching to my German congregation from Paul's charge to the elders at Ephesus: "I commend you to God and the word of His grace, which is able to build you up and give you an inheritance among them that are sanctified by faith that is in me." All were in tears, and praised God. Thus closed my work in Valparaiso. But I asked the question, "Will God ever bring me back?".

A Trip to the Old Fatherland.

Feb. 20. — Everything was now ready, and taking leave of many friends, we embarked for England that day. The steamer was about to sail, and the anchor was being heaved up, when in haste Dr. T. came on board, and handing me a check for forty-three pounds sterling, said that a friend on shore had given this for me, and I could get it cashed in England. Thus trusting God alone, we were supplied in time of need, just before sailing. Only fifteen minutes later and it would have been too late, for when the good Dr. descended the ladder, and touched the boat, the propeller made the first turn forward.

One Taken, the Other Left.

Bro. Collyer was to leave by sailing vessel soon after for California, his health failing rapidly. He looked much better than my wife, and the two, shaking hands, did not think, nor did any one else, that soon one was to be taken, and the other left. Bro. Collyer and wife embarked a few weeks after our departure, but on the way, out at sea, Jesus came and took him unto Himself, to be with Him for ever. When he prayed with me for the last time, till late in the night, for the life of my wife, and so wonderfully comforted me, I thought I had never seen Bro. C. so strangely filled with God. It was an hour in heaven as we talked together, and the will of God was made plain to me. One by one they are passing over. How long, O Lord! I wait for Thy appearing.

I now skip over my daily notes in the journal, as they would be of no interest to any one, being of almost continual sea-sickness, which besides kept me from keeping it perfectly. However, when in some port, I felt all right; or when passing the Straits of Magellan. I had hoped there to see some of the natives — Patagonians or Fuegians — but the weather being so rough, none dared to leave the dismal shore in their frail crafts. Little could be seen of the rocks or forests, being overhung with black clouds all the way to Sandy Point — the last Chilian port in the Straits.

THE METHODISTS IN URUGUAY AND THE ARGENTINE REPUBLIC.

From there we had a pleasant trip to Montevideo, Uruguay, on the East Coast. Going on shore, I visited the Methodist Missions. Rev. Mr. Wood had just left for the States on some business, but I met Mrs. W. and her children. She seemed an excellent lady, and full of work. I spent a pleasant hour with Rev. Mr. Talon, an ordained native minister, who told me much concerning the work in the city. I visited the church — an old theatre which had been bought and fitted up for an M. E. Church. It will seat from 500 to 550 people. The president of the Republic, a Roman Catholic, had contributed towards fitting up the chapel. At a recent meeting held there, 110 natives stood up, testifying for Christ; five of that number were students of the Buenos Ayres University (Argentine Republic), who, after they graduate, intend to enter the ministry of the M. E. Church. There I found, also, an extensive temperance work in progress, — a lodge of Good Templars, numbering about 150 members. Mrs. Wood had also a juvenile temperance lodge, numbering sixty boys and girls. A temperance boarding-house had been opened in connection with the lodge, which also paid twenty dollars per month towards the rent of the building. Three day-schools existed in connection with the Mission, and 600 children were taught in them. Five hundred of the number attend the Sabbath-school. Much pleased with my visit, I returned on board and then read Bishop Simpson's sermon, which he preached on the occasion of the Ecumenical Conference, held in London. It was a great blessing to me.

The ship left in the evening for Rio Janeiro. We had fine weather for a day, but then this terrible sea-sickness would come again, and I was unable to attend the service Sunday morning. The doctor on board told me it was very "nice," and remarked, "people are getting more educated now, and the clergy are at last compelled to write and read their sermons to keep them from rambling."

Rio Janeiro.

At 10 A. M., on Monday, we arrived in the harbor of Rio Janeiro — the most beautiful harbor in the world. Our little family could not resist the magnetic drawing toward the shore, and our little three-year old son clapped his little hands in delight when I told him, in English, that he should go with papa and mamma and little Herman Harris on shore; and running to his mother, he told her in German what I had said, and broke the glad news to his two-year old brother in Spanish. We visited Rev. Bro. Ransom, of the M. E. Mission South. They did good work in Rio, but not to the same extent as the brethren further south. The Methodists have a mission in the city, and another in the interior, and have in all about 120 members. The work is very hard here, and resembles much that in Chili. However, they have a good school. There is also a Seamen's Mission here. Our chief officer was taken sick suddenly while in the harbor, and had to be left in the hospital on shore, and the ship went on her journey without him. He died soon after; and before we reached our next and last port on the east coast of South America — Bahia. On the eighteenth of March we crossed the equator, and met five ships which worked to and fro on the little waves, apparently not moving a foot ahead. There was a dead calm.

March 23, we entered the harbor of St. Vincent, Cape de Verde Islands. Some six steamers were laying here,— French, English, German, and Italian, taking in coal.

Thursday, 27th, at 10 A. M., we sighted Teneriffe, one of the Canary Islands.

Saturday, March 31, dropped our anchor in the Bay of Lisbon, or rather in the river. Took in coal and started for Bordeaux. Across the Bay of Biscay we had the finest weather. I had formed the acquaintance of a young Roman priest, and I found him to be a most amiable companion in travel. He had left Lisbon because he had suffered some persecution on account of his liberal views in some matters of religion. He was certainly converted to God. He did not know that I was a Protestant missionary, and he spoke the more freely to me, and I enjoyed it very much to find him resting alone in Jesus. However, he leaned a little on the doctrine of works. Although he seemed to be free from anything like works without faith, he tried a little to hold up his church. The dear man, if he could only cut loose from everything but Jesus, he might be a useful man to lead sinners to repentance. He read with much interest the *Guide to Holiness*, and "Line and Plummet," and "Lessons in Holiness." In Bordeaux, my friend, the priest, went on shore.

Thirteen Years Ago an Infidel. — Days of Power in England.

April 7 we arrived safely in Liverpool, and with what feelings! As I stepped on shore with my dear wife and the children, I drew her close to my side, and when I was able to speak, I said to her: " Thirteen years ago I arrived in this city, on my way to the United States; but under what different circumstances! An infidel, fighting against everything that was good, without God and without hope. I had never touched a Bible." My wife understood me, and silently we stepped into a coach and drove to the hotel.

The following day I presented my letters of introduction to an English gentleman who has a business house in Valparaiso, and who did much to help us in establishing our Sailors' Home there. I was at once invited to another hotel by Mr. B., and after taking my family over, that gentleman called on me and informed me that Mr. Moody was in the city preaching. I was introduced to that great evangelist, whom I had longed to see and to hear. I was asked to take part in the work of the inquiry room, and I had occasion to see the work of the Lord for a fortnight. I was then invited by the Church of England Mission to Seamen to work for a time in Liverpool among the seafaring men. I accepted that call, and labored for twelve days, and

God seemed to continue here the work just left off in Valparaiso. I was interviewed by the managers of the Mersey Mission, and an offer was made me to enter the work in connection with that Mission and remain in Liverpool; but I would not accept it. My wife had had bleeding of the lungs, and on consulting the physicians they declared that the climate here would be injurious to her, and we had better leave for Germany at once. Many precious souls were converted during the four weeks of our stay in Liverpool. Praise God for His blessings!

I was invited to preach in a Baptist Church — to preach on holiness. After preaching, I invited those in the audience who wanted a clean heart " now," and while the congregation was singing a hymn, to come into the Sunday-School room, and I told them I would remain there on my knees praying for such until the room was full. I gave out the hymn, and then stepped down from the pulpit, and entered the small room back of the main hall. Then I knelt in prayer, and as the last notes of the hymn had passed away, the door opened and twenty-two persons, men and women, entered the room, and knelt all about me. Now the praying began,— one after another prayed for themselves. Then were confessions made, pardon asked, and prayers for clean hearts rose to God. It was remarkable how clear the prayers were. They evidently knew what they wanted. The meeting was entirely beyond human control,—the Spirit of God led the meeting. There was a sure basis to every prayer, and definitions were clear, and while they were praying and weeping, there was no confusion. All were blessed, and some while on their knees gave this testimony to the saving power of Jesus. A good number had been reclaimed from backsliding, others had been converted, and about seven testified clearly to heart purity. It was a meeting of power in this Baptist Church. I trust the blessed work will go on after I leave. The pastor is a live man, but a great "dipper." He came to my room before I left the city, and said: "If I accept this salvation, I am afraid my faith as a Baptist might be shaken." My answer was simple: "Dear sir, if God has given you light as to your own soul's salvation in connection with this requirement of 'holiness unto the Lord,' be sure to walk up to and in that light, and whatever God will tell you to do thereafter, you will know. He will never leave you nor forsake you. I have no commandment beyond that for you." He left me somewhat sorrowful.

Once more I preached at the Seamen's Bethel, in the afternoon, and seven men were happily converted to God. There were present at that meeting about fifty seamen. When about to leave the hall, a man much addicted to drink, came to me and wanted to sign the pledge. I pointed out to him the necessity of giving himself to Jesus. He promised to pray. Just then a sailor who had only just arrived from Bombay, came and desired to be prayed for "right now." When souls come like that, they shall surely find a ready Saviour; and he also was converted to God before leaving the room, and I was ready to remain all night, if necessary.

In another place where I had collected some men and women, God so wonderfully blessed the word that two women gave their hearts to Christ; another, who had said before the meeting began, "She did not want Christ," was melted to tears by what she saw; and being convicted, bewailed her own sins and was converted.

The day before leaving Liverpool for Hamburg was made a great blessing to me. I was invited to a sick clergyman of the Church of England, who lay at the "Bethshan," a faith-healing hospital. This man, I was told, had been afflicted with spinal disease for thirty-two years, and had not been able to preach, nearly always suffering acute pain, and unable to rise from his couch. I had never anything to do with faith-healing before this date; but when I was confronted by this poor suffering brother, and after consultation with him, he desired me that I would proceed according to the word in James — to anoint him with oil in the name of the Lord — and then added that he believed the Lord would heal him, I called in the members of the household, and we prayed. Then I anointed the brother in the name of the Lord, while the people were praying. The sufferer then tried to stir, but was wholly unable. He told me that he had more pains to-day than ever before, and he asked us to leave him, for he desired to be alone with God for a few hours. We retired. As I separated from the brethren and sisters, I exhorted them to pray. There was a meeting to be held in the evening, and they invited me to attend. I promised them to be present. I returned, but was a little too late; but what should I behold! The sick man was well, and had just opened the meeting by prayer, and was standing on his feet. "Praise God!" I cried, and caught his hand. "Yes, thanks be to God," said the brother, "God has done wonderful things for me." He then told his experience in the meeting. After we had left his room in the afternoon, he prayed to God, and said: "Yes, Lord, Thou dost heal me now!" and he sat up on the couch without any difficulty. Then he put one foot on the floor, and then the other, and felt no pain, "Then," said he, "I suddenly arose and stood on my feet, and clapping my hands, I praised God, and walked across the floor quite without pain — only felt a general weakness. The spinal disease, however, which has prostrated me these thirty-two years, has entirely disappeared." This was the Lord's doing, and it was wonderful in our eyes. (In 1884, since my return to Chili the second time, I received a letter in which this brother says : "*Dear Bro. K.*,— Thanks be to God, I am now back in active work, and able to preach twice on Sunday. God has completely healed me, and my body is getting stronger every day. My heart is full of gratitude. I shall print a tract concerning my deliverance, and spread it over the land. Yours in Jesus, B.")

May 2 we started for London, and remained two days there. On the street I met with so many seamen who had been converted in Valparaiso, it seemed as though they had congregated there. I was taken to some of the Mission Rooms established by Miss Weston, and there found myself surrounded by faces that I had been accustomed to see in South America, and I was so highly privileged to see what the Lord had wrought in the hearts of those men, who had come to Valparaiso in ships, and there, and on the way home, had been converted to God. I felt quite at home there, and preached several times, and some were converted in each meeting.

CHAPTER XIII.

ACROSS THE CHANNEL.—HOMEWARD BOUND.—THE REVIVAL IN GERMANY.

Sunday, the 6th of May, we were crossing the Channel on board the little steamer *Martin*, and here I wish to call the attention of the reader to my journal. I wish to copy the few lines following, from my journal, as I wrote them down on the morning of that memorable day. I hope it may help some one. May the dear Lord sustain me while, with a bleeding heart, I write down what now befell us, and God permitted to come upon us.

Heaviest Trials and Brightest Sunshine.

"*Pentecost Day.*—I pray for a special outpouring of God's Spirit upon my soul in view of the work before me. But in what wondrous way God will deal with me, I do not know now." These are the words as I copy them. This was done in the morning. Our dear children were enjoying themselves, running about and playing in the cabin. Mamma and papa were sea-sick most of the time, but it did not affect the children a moment. It was 6.15 P. M., when I noticed our youngest child, Herman Harris, two years old, looked tired, and was hanging his little head. He had just played with a gentleman, throwing slips of paper over a book he was reading, as he reclined on the sofa in the cabin. I thought the child was sleepy; so I went up to where the little fellow stood, and went to take him by the hand to lead him to his bed, when he began to vomit; at the same time our oldest boy came running to me, also vomiting. I supposed them to be seasick, and leading them back to the cabin where their mother lay, I said to her in a laughing way: "Here, mamma, our boys are sea-sick! What do you think?" Just then Herman dropped his head on his shoulder, and my wife, almost screaming, exclaimed: "Oh, just see how he turns his eyes! Give him to me, quick!" I lifted the boy up into the bed, and my wife received him into her arms. I called the captain and the stewardess at once. The captain just looked at the sick boy, and said: "He has the diphtheria — the worst kind!" Thick yellow slime then came out of nose and mouth. A warm bath with mustard was quickly prepared, but before he was put into the water, his eyes became glassy, his head and limbs hung lifeless. Yes, it was only too true — his spirit had fled. I held in my arms the lifeless body of our darling boy. Oh, how bitter! His merry laugh, we should hear it no more forever!

I copy from my journal again, the words that I wrote after the death of our darling: — "God knows best, yes, my soul says, God knows best — Father knows best — He doeth all things well. O Lord, my Father, I kiss thy hand to-night, for Thou can'st do but that which is good! Oh, the comfort of Thy living presence! Teach me the lesson of this solemn hour, my God and my Father! Oh, the power of Jesus! Oh, His wondrous love! My soul is saturated with His love, and peace fills my heart — a peace that floweth like a river, — yes, saturated with Thy love, O God! Praises belong to Thee!"

Early in the morning of the following day — Monday, the fifth, — we arrived in Hamburg. Our boy had been lying in a state-room; from time to time during the night I would go and kneel beside the corpse and kiss the sweet face and call his name. At times it seemed to me as though I saw his breast heave; but it was not true, he had gone to heaven. I cannot understand to this day how he was taken from us; but I know and say this: God took him. His little body was laid in a coffin and was bedded in flowers, then he was taken on shore. My wife had become like a shadow in appearance, pale and care-worn. I durst not ask her anything, but she gave me to understand that the heavy hand resting on her was the hand of Omnipotence. Our Eugene, now our only boy, had also taken sick, and the captain had told us to send for a good physician at once. So we went to a hotel and a good medical man was secured, who stated that the throat of the boy was very bad; but he might recover. What did God desire to do with us?

Tuesday morning.— Our Eugene is getting worse, and the Dr. thinks an operation is necessary. In the afternoon the body of our youngest child was committed to the earth. At 12 P. M., Eugene was taken to the hospital of one of the best physicians of Hamburg, who would perform the operation. It was successful, and the following day we were permitted to see our child. Oh, what prayer arose to God! Only One can understand, in this hour of bitter trial, the language of our hearts, and to Him we go and wait, sitting at His feet and looking into His blessed face, watching any sign as to what He will decide. Sweetest comfort and sweetest assurance, shined from the face of the Son of God, into our poor smitten hearts, and we said: "As Thou wilt, Lord." More we were not able to say; but we wept, yes, bitterly we wept. As my poor wife held the child she loved so much, in her arms, we did scarcely recognize him. Then the Dr. came and told us we must go. One last kiss, one last look upon our last hope, and we left. We had just arrived at the hotel, when a messenger arrived about the same time, who brought the news that this, our sweet boy, had also departed out of the world, soon after we left his bedside.

My Children Both Gone to be with Jesus.

I now draw a curtain. We want to be alone and shut out the world from this scene of our grief,—alone with God,—to be still, and drink, and drink, and drink, to cool our parching tongues, and satisfy the longing of our souls, at the fountain. "They shall never come back to us; but we shall go to them." Yet, whom have I in heaven but Thee? As the sad news came to us, I pressed her, who alone was left to me on earth, to my aching heart. Our eyes met, and once more these words burst from our lips: "They shall never come back to us, but we shall go to them." "The Lord has given; the Lord has taken away; blessed be the name of the Lord."

Friday, May 11, our Eugene was buried — sleeping in flowers, which he loved so much when in life. He had been a sweet boy. How often did he throw aside his playthings, and running in, he would take his mamma's hand, and leading her into the parlor, he would say: "Now, mamma, come pray with me," and he prayed for such as he had met through the day, and then closed with, "God bless papa! God bless mamma! Amen!" He has gone to be a jewel in the crown of our Redeemer. My wife had asked him before the operation took place: "Will you go away?" "Yes, mamma, I shall go." Then, awaking, he said (in

German): "Hallelujah! God, my Father!" We had never used just these words in his presence, so far as we can remember, and they startled us when we heard them from his lips. The death of our darling, — was it necessary? I think not; but the Lord certainly permitted it. May all redound to His glory!

The following Sunday night I passed through a wonderful experience. Oftentimes during the night I awoke out of sleep, and found myself clapping my hands and praising God aloud. My wife was wonderfully sustained. We were swallowed up of life.

May 12, we left Hamburg, and arrived soon at the home of my aged father; but as he looked about him to see the grand-children, we had to tell him: "They have gone to heaven. You cannot see them now."

At the Grave of my Sainted Mother.

May 19, we visited the grave of my dear mother. Oh, how I should have loved to meet her on earth! When eleven years ago Jesus saved my soul, I sat down and wrote: — "*Dear Mother,* — Your boy has found Jesus." When she died, she said: "If only my boy could be here!" As I stood at the grave, once more the past rose up before me, and I wept there. I saw a single forget-me-not on the grave, and I plucked it. Then I turned away, but I felt in my soul, and confessed with my mouth: "We shall meet beyond the river by and by. We have anchors over there."

I visited then the old church where I had been confirmed — not knowing Jesus the Saviour; but now, what a contrast! then a sinner lost through sin; now a sinner saved through grace — made a minister and a witness for Jesus. As I stood on the spot where I had bowed my head seventeen years ago to receive the blessing pronounced upon me by the officiating minister, it brought up to my view the moment when Bishop Harris laid his hands upon me, and ordained me an elder in the Methodist Episcopal Church, in which Church I had found my Saviour and Redeemer. These remembrances of the past were a balm to my soul, and my dear wife understood me so well, and with tearful eyes, but thankful heart, she praised the good Redeemer's love. God is good.

I received an invitation now to come to Berlin, from Count B. and Count P., to open evangelistic services and preach to the masses of the unconverted, and for that purpose rent halls, theatres, and such places, easy of access to the people. I accepted the invitation, and we started for Berlin on the second of June.

Preaching in Berlin.

The first meeting was attended by 350 persons, in a hall which was formerly used for dancing; but had been bought by Christian workers for Christian work. The plan of the inquiry-room was here adopted, but few persons could be induced to come; however, my private dwelling was crowded. Seekers of pardon and purity came to my room day by day, and the work of salvation began at once. Several were converted after the first meeting, and the outlook was favorable. A woman came to my house, who had been trying hard to get peace by attending all the means of grace regularly; but had never succeeded. But now she sought forgiveness of sin, and abhorred it. Meetings were now arranged for, and two meetings appointed each day at 3 P. M., and 8 A. M., and in different parts of the city. Suitable halls were rented to accommodate from 300 to 800 persons. The halls were always filled with anxious hearers.

THE POWER OF LOVE.

A lady came to me in great distress, and having heard a sermon on holy living, desired to be made clean. She was determined not to leave the room without the clean heart. She said she had a wayward daughter, who would seek unfit company, and go out dancing. She had tried everything, and also scolded her often, and nothing would help. I had no doubt about it; but when the mother left the house, praising the Lord for a clean heart, she said: "Pray for my daughter." A few days after the interview, the same woman stood up in a meeting and told what God had done for her and her daughter: "I thank God He has given me a clean heart, and has taken away this bad temper which I used to have. I often wondered why I could do nothing for my daughter; but to-day I know. Yesterday she did not come home till late, but I sat up and waited for her. I felt I loved my daughter as I never had before. I had kept her supper warm — a thing I never thought of before, and I prayed until she came. Opening the door for her, I invited her to sit down, and I spread the table, and placed before her something to eat. I sat opposite to her. My daughter could not eat; she put down her knife and fork, and hiding her face in her hands, wept bitterly. I then got up, and putting my arm around her, kissed her. She then looked at me, and said: 'Mother, what is the matter with you? I cannot bear this.' 'My dear girl, God has filled my heart with love'; and we got on our knees together, and she gave her heart to God. She could stand all my scolding and talking for years, but she could not stand against love. Oh praise God for a baptism of love!"

Sunday, July 29, the Lord so powerfully blessed the preaching of the word, that the people could not leave the room, but where they sat they knelt and prayed, so that I was compelled to have an after-meeting, notwithstanding the opposition on the part of my friends, who called me to the work. We could not, possibly, throw the seekers out of the hall. The Germans here are much afraid of anything that looks Methodistic, or is indicative of excitement; and the work is somewhat hard under the circumstances. But the Lord is leading, as in this case to-night. A prostitute was converted to God, and afterward entered an institution to become a worker for God. A man and wife sought pardon and were blessed, and one sister found the clean heart. The word of God spread in a remarkable manner. Souls were saved every day, and at every meeting that was held. The Sankey hymns, translated into German, had a wonderful effect on the people, and they fell in love with them. In each meeting I taught them some new hymns, and they learned surprisingly fast. It put new fire into our service, and hardened sinners were convicted for sin and came confessing their sins. With most of those who were converted, I had an opportunity to converse, as they came to my house and room, and there prayed with me.

A Remarkable Feature.— Confession of Sins.

Something in this work was comparatively new to me; it was that those who came to me felt that they must confess their sins, no matter what they were, and in each case I saw them entering the blessing of pardon or heart purity. I had those who kept back their sins for hours, and were not relieved until they confessed. It was terrible how Satan had precipitated souls into sin and vice in this great city. Crimes of all sorts were shamelessly committed by males and females, but the power of God was so revealed to their souls, that, broken up and in tears, they would often come from the streets, and confessing their sins, obtain pardon from God. In this way, liars, thieves, burglars and pickpockets, and prostitutes, came and found peace, and I could easily see which conversions were genuine, and which were not. The struggle seemed fearful in some cases, so that it was very trying work to me, because of the feeling of sympathy that would go out from me for them; but the Lord gave me strength for that kind of work, and blessed me much in preaching — plain preaching. I seemed to have to do with the offscouring of society, and they came to Jesus.

A lady came convicted for sin. She said: "I am so fond of dancing and the theatre, and the concert-garden; and last night God brought me to see my sins. The devil told me I could never give up the world, and that the Christian life is a hard life; but I come to confess my sins and receive forgiveness for Jesus' sake. I believe Christ will save me and keep me."

I had now established private-house meetings in many families. Those who were converted led the meetings, and such as had been convicted, not only came to my house, but attended these meetings, which were held every afternoon, in different parts of the city, — these, answering in a measure for the inquiry-room, and were the means of doing incalculable good; many being converted to God, and believers built up, and there these souls were taught to confess their Saviour and pray in public. These meetings became so popular that, in order that this blessed work might be extended, separate organizations took place. These were young ladies' meetings, women's meetings, and meetings for men, and in these meetings we had conversions daily.

A Daughter Brings Home Her Wandering Parents.

One young lady who had given herself over to the world was brought to Christ, and her mother tells me the following: "My daughter came home after one of the meetings, and I saw her manner had altered. When supper was served she sat down at the table and wept. I then spoke to her, thinking she was ill. She kissed me and her father, and begged us to permit her to ask the blessing at the table, and after supper she took up our old Bible, which had not been used for years, and we had family worship. She read and prayed. Oh, how I bless God that my daughter has found the Saviour! it has been the means of bringing us to Christ." Thus may a daughter confess Jesus in the family, and God will honor it, as in this case. When Peter was ashamed of Jesus, he fell; when he confessed the Saviour, he was blessed. "Blessed art thou!" thus Christ pronounced the blessing upon the apostle, and upon this confession He will build His church.

While in Berlin, the people among themselves collected the money to pay the rents of our halls, which were hired for preaching; and never was I in debt, although the rents were often high. The self-supporting plan worked here, as well as in Chili, and I believe it does the same in all the world. I had never to ask for any help — it came in according to our needs. The redeemed of the Lord collected money in the private meetings, and putting it in an envelope, sent it to me, or hid it in my Bible, or in some way made me the recipient without my knowing whence it came. One day I found $15 between the leaves of my Bible. Some one, prompted by the Spirit, had placed it there. Others made it a rule to send a certain sum every month; but in such cases I would know only the person that gave me the collection, in case it was handed to me in person. Our expenses were high while we lived in Berlin, for we were compelled to board; but after paying our bill every month, there was always some "oil" left in the cruise. We never, at any time, ran dry.

A mother came to pray with me for her lost daughter. She had been away for two years. I wrote a note in my journal, and the date on which prayer was made.

Three days after, the mother came with a letter in hand, and while the tears of joy flowed freely, she read it to me. The lost daughter had written and asked: "Dear mother, will you forgive your daughter that has grieved you so much, since God has been merciful to me, and has forgiven me? and may I come home?" I asked this woman: "And what will you tell her?" "Oh, that I forgive her, of course, and to come home at once!" Is not this the Father's way, if a poor sinner comes? Of course He will forgive, and is waiting for the weary one to come home. Is not the parable of the prodigal verified in thousands of households all over the world, and is God not true? Another lady had taken a sister, who was entirely given to the world, to the meetings. She was happily converted while listening to the preaching, while she who had brought her there, was not converted. She thought herself already "good," and when she saw the joy of her sister, there was a strange feeling of jealousy manifested, and the poor girl seemed quite hardened after that. But God kept the saved one. Every day, now, I received one or more letters from such as had accepted the Saviour at their homes; and these letters were above a hundred, ringing with the sweetest testimonies. However, some there were who felt to confess the Lord by letter, and were afraid to confess because of "friends" (?)

Ashamed of Christ.

In the meetings I spoke to such, or rather, about such, not mentioning names, of course; telling them God would not honor such a confession, and that they had better throw off the bushel, or else they might soon go back to the world. Ashamed of Christ! There are many who would like to "permit" Christ to save them from their dirty sins, but they will have hard times. They would very much like to be His servants, but not wear the livery. Ashamed of the livery of heaven! yet they will go on wearing a mask, and everybody knows. Thousands are outside, weeping like Peter, and thousands have dried their tears, and are not returned, — they find out that to retain salvation, means to "confess Christ."

A sister came to see me. She was full of joy, and said: "I thought you should be partaker of my joy, and so I tell you that God, for Christ's sake, has forgiven me all my sins." What a sweet sound confession is. We were both blessed, and while talking, a young man came in and stood weeping. He was hungering and thirsting for Christ. "All this week," he said, "I have been in this condition, and the enemy has kept me from coming to speak with you; but I thank God that I am here. Will you pray with me?" We then prayed, and the poor lost one prayed, and found his Christ before leaving the room.

An infidel came to the night meeting, and afterwards came to ask for a Bible "for his wife" (?) With a prayer to God to bless the reading of the word to his own soul, a copy was given to him. Three souls were converted in the meeting. A woman who once had loved the Lord, came back to God after long years of bitter life. She said: "I married an ungodly man, but at the time, I thought he might be converted; but I was bitterly disappointed, and gradually I have fallen back myself. Soon I was no better than he. Thank God! I am saved now." A young lady has no business to let herself go so far as to love an ungodly man, enough to marry him. God's girls need to move up closer to Jesus when they find it out, and pray for deliverance — either in the conversion of the man, or the sanctification of their own hearts; for surely there is something wrong, because God does not agree with us. 2 Cor. vi. 14, and 1 Cor. xi. 30. Then these poor, deceived souls, think they "backslide," while really, they have not "slid forward" in time of their greatest need. Some have waited till their husbands or wives died, and then were converted. So in the case of this woman. They look back upon the lost years — a wasted life — and the last snuff of an expiring candle is offered to the Lord. When Joshua was commanded to lead the children of Israel over Jordan, he was told to observe the law of God. "Turn not thou to the right or to the left, that thou mayest prosper whithersoever thou goest." It pays to take time to consult the word of God. A moment with God saves us an eternity of misery and remorse.

After one of the evening meetings, my soul was much burdened for certain ones whom I knew to be convicted; and coming home, I could not eat nor drink, and in the morning I felt the same. And so I bowed in prayer, and knew that I should remain there, fasting and praying, and said: "Father, I cannot arise until the door opens and these precious souls come in." I knelt there until 10 o'clock, A. M.; then all was bright and clear. The burden had rolled away, and I could only praise God, but still on my knees. Then I heard the bell ringing, and there were two; but not only they who had been long convicted, but others came and sought the Lord. After the first two, others followed, and all that day men and women came and went. A wonderful day! Some had been too troubled the night before to go to sleep, and in the morning they could find no peace until they sought it at Jesus' feet.

At a meeting in the afternoon, at 3.30, three souls remained in the hall and were converted, and four more at another meeting at six o'clock, before the preaching service in the large hall. A man living in adultery came, and, confessing his sin, obtained forgiveness. The following day he brought his poor, unhappy wife, who had almost despaired of ever being happy any more, and then it seemed as if new life had entered their souls, and, like as twenty years ago, when they knelt at the altar together, a purer and a nobler union was established between them. Yes, the life of Christ was theirs from that moment. (Since my return to South America, I received a letter from this family. They established a weekly meeting at their house, and to this day it is kept up, and God blesses them in the work of winning souls.)

The Experience of a Dressmaker.

A dressmaker who had received money from many ladies to put "extras" on dresses, which "mother" did not order, and who in many cases confessed that the money had been obtained under rather doubtful circumstances, was so troubled about receiving such money, that after hearing the word, she must confess her sins to God, and was happily converted. She said then: "My work is all among the better class; but, oh," said she, "you would be surprised how many of the most refined daughters of the best families commit this sin, and I believe mothers themselves, who wish so much that their daughters may look nice and neat, train them to steal money out of father's or mother's pocketbook; and they do not suspect at all what harm they are doing by encouraging fashion." I do not doubt it a moment. Does it not remind one of the "chain-gang" already, to hear the tinkling of arm-bands of to-day on the wrists of the fair daughters of the land. This woman gave back the money she had of late received. The parties were ashamed and thunderstruck by her simple testimony for Jesus, and she lost her customers; but she told me she got so much to do, as to occupy her all day. Others had been sending her work who would not steal from their fathers and mothers.

SNATCHED FROM THE BURNING.

A poor girl, who was persecuted by a German baron, came bitterly weeping, to seek the Saviour. She had just heard God's word, and it fastened in her heart like an arrow; and when the tempter came, she fled from him. She could not sleep all the night following. She could but weep. God had preserved her from a dreadful fall. She came in the morning and said: " I must pray with you. I must find my Saviour this morning." I pitied her as she wept. It seemed there was something so dreadful about her trouble, and she manifested a dread to leave the room, and she would say: "I cannot go on the street without my Saviour: no, I will not! I will not! I must have Christ!" I said: " Tell me what is in the way. You must be calm for a moment, and look to Christ, and He will save your soul, and your tormenting fears will all be gone." She sat down and seemed calm for a few minutes, and she said: " He will come back again to-day, and I see my awful sinfulness and weakness. I must be God's this moment." She had become quite calm, and I could speak to her. She saw now clearly what she wanted, and in deep humiliation she lay at the feet of Jesus, and then the peace that filled her soul was wonderful. It was pictured on her face. She praised God for salvation through Christ. I met this person afterwards, and she said God had arranged everything wonderfully for her, and had spared her the bitter struggle of the meeting she had anticipated in the morning of her deliverance. The baron had fled to Italy, involved in other troubles. God delivereth the poor and needy, and them that cry unto Him. Glory be to God forever!

A few days after this occurrence, the lady brought her sister to the meetings, and she was converted to God, and leads a young ladies' meeting. Two women came to me for prayer and salvation. They had both lived in open rebellion against God and the laws of the country; but eight years ago they had heard the word, and they were afraid to go on in sin. They concluded to leave the path of unrighteousness, and provide honestly for themselves in the sight of man and God, and attend church every Sunday. "For eight years we have been miserable," they said, " our conscience smote us all this time, and there was no peace within us. We tried everything to do right; but we have no peace with

God. We have attended the meetings in the city, and now see what we really want. We must be born again." I prayed with them, and they both prayed for themselves, and before leaving me, had found what they had not found in all the eight years of trying to work out this salvation, when nothing was "in" to "work out,"— the pardon of their sin and the cleansing from indwelling sin. They knew all about the "repression theory,"— they had tried their hand at that these many years, and I could easily lead them immediately from pardon to purity. They saw their privileges in Christ, and accepted Him as their Justifier and Sanctifier by faith.

I had preached on Rom. viii. 1. The following morning the postman brought me two letters from such as had, during the night, at home, found perfect love, and felt constrained to confess at once by letter. Another person came to my room, and there found perfect rest from inbred sin.

A mother brought her two children and a friend, all adults. The mother stepped into an adjoining room to pray there alone, while the three remained with me. Soon light came, and the son ran to meet his mother, and kissing her affectionately, cried out: "It is all right now, mother! I am saved from sin!" So, also, testified the other two, and it was a great blessing to my own heart to see those three happy souls, just saved, and a mother who saw her children brought to Christ. Also, that day, I received twelve letters bringing the glad news that as many souls had found the Saviour.

Sept. 6, took train for Z——, East Prussia, to hold a ten days' meeting, together with more friends from the south of Germany.

Satan on Development.

First meeting, two souls remained after the meeting, and were converted to God. They were man and wife. Both had stood on the ground of "development" for years; but found they had not developed out of sin yet, and let Christ save them. Satan likes this developing idea very much, and does not mind it if a person only stays there a good long time, in not believing that Christ can save from sin "now." This "to-day,"— if he could only scratch it out of the Bible, he would do good business, and hell would enlarge her borders.

The meetings at Z—— were of great good. People from far and near attended the meetings, and these were a great blessing to the whole community. Many were converted to God. The wife of a clergyman could not find forgiveness, although praying with tears and in great agony. I discovered that she would not forgive some people who had sinned against her and her husband, speaking evil, and, as she thought, had neglected him in a severe sickness. So God could not forgive her. She went away sorrowful, but unsaved.

Returning to Berlin, the meetings were continued. I attended a lecture given by an infidel. He said among other foolish things concerning the development of lower life into higher life: "The eel will leave his watery bed and go into a field of green peas, of which he is very fond, and thus take upon him the nature of a snake; or the robber-bee goes out and robs the beehives from an instinct, trusting to make an easier living, and develop a higher species of their kind." I left the place, and thought, the convicts in the penitentiary would not agree with him there. With them it has proved only true, in the development of a higher species of their kind,— robbers, murderers, etc. But as man? Here is Christ, who can save, change from glory to glory, as by the Spirit of the Lord.

A REMARKABLE EXPERIENCE IN FASTING.

A man who had developed into a lower species of his kind through drink, was brought to God, and in this wise: A woman came to me and requested prayer for her husband, who had been eight years a drunkard. I discovered that this praying wife was a most excellent Christian, tried in the fire of affliction; but kept humble, and endued with wonderful patience. Patience had had her perfect work in her in the highest sense of the word. Not a cross word, on her part, with her husband all these years. She nursed him like a child, and cared for him as a wife only can, and yet no change. We prayed for the poor drunkard, and taking up the Bible, I read to the woman: "This cometh not out but by prayer and fasting." She looked at me for a moment, and I told her it had just occurred to me, that along with the prayers there was another way opened, and as up to date everything had failed, then the Lord opened a way, left untried. This she listened to eagerly. She seemed to drink in every word, and a new light had dawned upon her. Then she said: "But how will I fast? My husband, if he sees I will not eat at the table with him, may get angry." "Dear sister," I said, "I would not dare make a commandment for you, and it would never do to make any arrangement with me here; but you go to your home and pray, and let God direct you about it." "But how will I know?" "Just go now and you shall know. God will remove every doubt about the matter, if this be the way for you to go." She left me. After eight days she came back, and looked so happy and fresh. Her eyes were not red, and the careworn look was not upon her face. She said: "My soul exalteth God for His wonderful mercy. When I returned home, I retired and prayed much to God for His divine direction in regard to my husband, and to my great grief he came home that night intoxicated, and in the morning was unable to rise, he was sick. It had now become clear to me I could fast unhindered. I attended him all day, but he did not speak to me. When dinner came I fasted, and when supper came I fasted; but before going to bed I felt sick, and oh, so faint! I craved something to eat. I knelt down in prayer for my husband, and while pleading with God, I received a baptism which I had not had before, and when I arose I had no desire for food; and it did not come back, although I fasted all the next day also, even not taking any water to drink. My husband got very much worse, and I begged him to send for a doctor; but he would get angry when I mentioned it to him. He would not speak to me, and gave me no answer to anything I asked him, and this was a sore trial; but I was much strengthened in prayer. The third day came, and he felt very sick, and I still fasted and prayed. I knew I had hold of Christ for my husband, and would not let go until He would answer me. That day I knew that God would save my husband. When evening came he sent for me. He called me by name, which he had not done for a long time. I had to restrain myself to keep from weeping. I sat down on the bed, and stroked his burning forehead. He took my hand, and for the first time for years I saw him shedding tears. Then he asked me to forgive him; I knelt down beside the bed and held his dear hand in mine, and kissed him. I forgave him everything with all my heart. He then said, 'Oh that God might forgive me!' Now the Lord's time had come, and we prayed together. He gave up the cup from that hour, and we are happy once more, after eight years wandering. My husband is happy, and I am happy." She closed her affecting story by saying: "I have seen the glory of my God. Thanks be to Jesus, the mighty Saviour!"

A young merchant, who had been completely captured by the theatre and fashion-devil, followed me in the cars four miles after a meeting, and then, at my house, spoke to me, and asked me, with tears in his eyes, not to part with him until he had found the Saviour. He spoke so touchingly, that I could not refrain from embracing him, and weeping with him. He came to my room with me, and there prayed, and God was merciful to this dear man. A portrait painter, in the same way, was brought to Jesus.

When Christmas came, I was surprised in a very pleasant manner. Those who had been converted in Berlin, conspired with my good wife to make me a nice present, and had asked her to give them one of our pictures. Christmas eve it was returned, and when I stepped into the room, I saw before me, in a beautiful frame, and under glass, a fine picture of myself and wife, five feet high. Our young painter did the work in crayon. This was a great surprise indeed. It did me much good to see the good will of those who had so recently given their hearts to God.

About this time the Lord was working in saving power among the young men, and a large number were converted, and with these several Sunday-schools were opened in different parts of the city, and now our evangelistic meetings were opened in the same parts of and the city, conducted under remarkable signs of God's favor.

The meetings now reminded me much of the times and seasons of special refreshing in the United States, such as I so often experienced during camp-meetings and revivals. Men and women were so powerfully wrought upon by the Spirit, that they could not leave the house after preaching. The "church" was much opposed to the idea of a revival, or after-meetings; but the people would not go home, and I was willing that God should have His way about it; and so, many who had been saved through grace, were ready for work, and did work. In a meeting which I held in a new district, God so blessed the people that all over the hall they were kneeling, seeking for God, and all the workers had work, praying with the seekers. Every chair was turned into an altar, and scores of precious souls were being saved. It was 11.30 when the lights were put out that evening.

During the following day my house was filled with

such as would seek the Lord; continually going and coming, and the most remarkable conversions took place. A poor sin-stricken woman came and confessed that two years ago she had told lies at court, in order to save her brother from degradation; but she could not rest since the word had been preached to her. The poor soul struggled hard, and the enemy seemed to have a particularly good servant in her. The lying devil is a mean devil, and hangs to men and women longest of anything else. God deliver the millions of the earth from lies! They believe lies, and tell lies. God have mercy!

CHAPTER XIV.

EAST PRUSSIA. — THE ANCIENT CITY OF THE KINGS.

For the month of January I was invited to labor in East Prussia. I started for Elbing on the second, and an eighteen hours ride by rail brought me to the city. At 8 P. M., next day, I preached to an immense congregation in the largest hall of the city, from the text in Matthew xii. 45, 46, — "the costly pearl." The religion of Jesus Christ is worth more than anything else in the world. It is like unto a merchantman seeking pearls, when he has found one of great price he selleth all that he hath to be the possessor. Can there be anything said to exceed this saying of our Master as to the worth of possessing Christ? Three persons came to my room next day. One had been disappointed in his worldly career, had not sought after goodly pearls, but labored to find the counterfeit pearls. Another feared the terrors of death, and the third found it hard work to carry the world under one arm, and religion under the other. Poor soul! he was tired out, and weary of this life. "Sell all," and possess the pearl of highest price. How many labor for that which satisfieth not! Poor Agrippa, with his crown! "Almost thou persuadest me," — he had not the pearl. Who was the real king? — Agrippa, with the crown upon his brow, or Paul, with the iron chain upon his wrists? Ahab in his marble palace, or the prophet before him, in camels-hair dress? The rich man, faring sumptuously — surrounded by the luxuries and comforts of life, — or poor Lazarus, with the dogs licking his sores? No! no! we cannot be mistaken in the answer.

Sunday, Jan. 6, was a day of special outpouring of the the Holy Ghost. It was the last day of meeting with the people in this city. Scores had found the Saviour, and especially among the young people a blessed work was in progress. Three meetings had been held each day through the week, and at every meeting the Lord saved some. At 2 P. M., I called a children's meeting. The large hall was crowded,— not a vacant place to be found. I spoke to them on John xiv. 1, 2. It seemed heaven on earth to be with these dear little lambs. At 4 P. M., meeting for adults. Preached on the five "cities of refuge." This meeting was one of great power. The 8 P. M. meeting was still more so. Preached on "Abraham and Lot," or the difference between him that serveth God, and him that serveth him not. Many found Christ on that memorable evening, and I bade them farewell.

In the Right Spirit.

The Countess v. G. of P——, had invited me to preach in that place, and given two large halls in her mansion for that purpose. I accepted the invitation, and started for P——, Monday forenoon. Every preparation had been made and the people invited for the first meeting at 5 P. M., of the same day. The house was filled with anxious hearers, and God condescended to pour out the spirit of conviction at the start, so that many felt constrained to inquire the way of salvation. The countess had been much in England, and was well acquainted with the modes of work during the Moody meetings, and so I had no trouble in inviting the people to the different adjoining apartments, turning them into inquiry rooms, and the countess as well as a sister of hers proved valuable helpers with the seekers. I followed the programme of the Evangelical Alliance, which was now in session all over the world. That spirit of union was felt in a remarkable degree in all the meetings of the week. A deaconess of the Lutheran Church in that place entered the inquiry room, and found a perfect salvation from all sin, by accepting sanctification by faith, thus fitting her for work in the inquiry room. The second day, seven souls rushed into the inquiry room; they were in great haste to get rid of sin and Satan. All prayed, and hearts were searched, and confessions of sin made to the Lord. There was great joy in the house that day. God had surely visited His people. The holiness meetings in the afternoons proved to be of vital importance. God seemed then to prepare us for the work before us, and we were not mistaken. While many in these meetings were led to a full and complete surrender, and the undecided led to decision, we found that the presence of the Spirit of God, in the evangelistic services for the unconverted, was manifested in great power, and when the work began among the seekers, the Lord's people were ready for it. They did not then come to "claim faith," but they came to "exercise faith;" and not so much "to be helped" themselves, as to "help others." Thus our minds were bent on this one object, that God might be glorified so that we bear much fruit. There were no different desires among the workers — we kept the "unity of the faith," and we understood this, and each other. Thus the powers of darkness gave way, and Christ was conqueror, and the recipients of His grace more than conquerors through Him that saved them from all sin. The meetings closed Sunday evening, Jan. 13; but to the last night the inquiry room was filled with seekers. Seven of the servants in this house had been converted to God, and the last man was the gardener, who had been addicted to drink, and came near losing his situation on that account. He settled the question forever by coming to Jesus, and was accepted a member of the heavenly family. It was a blessing to me to see with my eyes how his Christian wife, who had been praying for him these many years, was filled with joy, and wept for joy on the neck of her husband.

The next station where meetings had been announced, and hall rented, was was Heiligenbeil. The hall was rather crowded, and some chairs and benches were taken out to give standing room. The Spirit of God had stirred the country round about, and fell in power upon them when the word was preached. I arrived at 6 P. M., and preached at 7 P. M., so I drove from the station immediately to the hall. The people were burning to hear the word.

A Methodist Old-Fashioned Meeting.

Forty seekers remained after the meeting, and as we had no smaller rooms there, the brethren arranged an altar for the mourners. It was a good old-fashioned Methodist mourners' bench, but I had no time, however, to give it a name, or to explain. It was soon crowded, and the workers at work. One after another of the seekers arose, and confessed the Saviour. Such a meeting I had not seen for a long time: so many in one place praying to God for pardon. Not a soul was left behind,— all had found the Saviour. The enemy had been totally surprised and defeated; but he tried a game. The hall-owner informed the committee after the meeting, that the hall could not be had for other meetings. We did not attempt to hold him to his contract, but before leaving the house, another man, having heard of it, came and offered his house without money and without price. The Lord opened a door, and who shall shut it? Never fear, little flock — the Lord is thy Shepherd. The following evening was the last meeting in this place, and seven others stood up before the close, and confessed the Saviour.

Wednesday, 16th, proceeded to a farm-house in the country; but the accommodations were too small. It being winter, I thought it must be very uncomfortable to those standing in the halls and doors; but they would rather remain than to go away. Now, to describe this meeting, would be utterly impossible. Among the number that here found Jesus was one young man who found the Saviour in entire sanctification after he had been reclaimed from a cold, half-alive condition. While he praised God on his knees, he prayed God to help him to be true to his conviction to preach the Gospel, when a wealthy farmer's wife said: " Yes, amen, and I will pay his way." Would to God more such women and men would say such "amens" with a substantial backing to it. Many, however, like to say amen while others are praying, and never think that God wants them to answer that prayer. They expect it from elsewhere.

Thursday, left for Bladieu, a town not far away. When I arrived in the afternoon, I found the people waiting, and Satan, too, had come to do his work; but we will see how the dear Lord stood by us. The meeting had been announced for seven o'clock, but the people had crowded the large hall ever since four in the afternoon. Carts and wagon-loads full of human freight were lining the streets on every side, and hundreds on foot crowded the entrance to the house. The hall was upstairs, and used for dancing when it was secured for our meeting. When time for meeting had come, several brethren accompanied me, and, as they said, "to make room for me to go up stairs." I let them work for awhile, but, bathed in perspiration, they came back and had not succeeded in clearing a passage, and there seemed a great noise in the hall upstairs. I asked the brethren to wait and see how the Lord would help. So I raised my voice above the din, and cried: "Friends! I am here, and come to preach; just make room." In an instant the passage was cleared, and I was lifted up, and quicker than I ever got upstairs anywhere, I was set down inside the hall.

Satan had sent some of his agents to work to frustrate our efforts that evening. Some infidels had collected together and offered to pay for a barrel of beer, if certain individuals, who now were trying to raise a disturbance upstairs, should succeed in stopping the progress of the meeting. The people had removed every chair and every bench, and even my table, from the room, and lifted the doors out of their hinges, leading into other rooms adjoining our hall; and thus tried to make more room; but I thought they must feel uncomfortable, and would hurt our meeting. However, as I gave out the hymn: " There is a fountain filled with blood," I felt the Spirit's presence.

Rioters made Friends.

Reading the hymn, five drunken men,—those hired for the occasion,—kept up a great noise, and began quarrelling with those around them, and used profane language. The people became restless, and seeing this, I commanded the brethren to pray, while I turned to those rough men and said to them: "Now, friends, I want to teach you this beautiful new hymn. I'll sing a verse. Now, watch and catch the tune." There was a dead silence in an instant, and I sang the first verse of that powerful hymn, with the chorus, " I do believe, I now believe." My five men, who had crowded about me, sang now the loudest, as I raised my finger asking all to join me in repeating the verse. Then I asked all the females to sing the same verse, and the men join in the chorus. When the latter did so, I saw two of the would-be disturbers make their way out of the hall, making an effort to leave unnoticed, but I saw them. The other two mixed up with those standing about and sang, and when the last verse was sung, one of the poor fellows wept like a child. Then followed the sermon. I stood on a small soap-box against the wall, but the Lord was there, and the word was wonderfully blessed to the hearers. It came down into their hearts in Pentecostal power. I preached from Ezek. xviii, 20: " The soul that sinneth, it shall die." Near the close of the discourse I was constrained to cry out: "Who will take life?" In an instant about thirty hands were up. It was of God, and I asked them to remain in that position until I counted them, in order to pray with them. Scarcely had I used the word "pray" when everybody knelt down, and the cries of those who desired life rose up to Heaven. Quickly the forces were collected and set to work, to help those dear souls in praying to God and pointing them to the Lamb of God.

The Day of Pentecost had Fully Come.

When the meetings closed, there were so many who had not been able to hear the word, I felt sorry for them; they seemed to be hungering. I invited them for to-morrow, when three meetings were to be held. The house was filled to overflowing, and several meetings had to be held in succession. In the evening meeting, which was to be the last, I preached from Acts xxvi.: "Almost thou persuadest me to be a Christian." In the midst of the discourse I was interrupted by those who sought the Lord. It was time to go to work among them as the night before, and God was there to save. At 9 P. M., by the help of the brethren, we cleared the hall, so as to open a second meeting, and admit those who had been waiting in the street — standing in the snow. I preached from 2 Cor. x.: "Be ye reconciled to God." The same power was manifested as in the first meeting. Some were praying aloud in the adjoining rooms, and others in the hallway leading down stairs. By this time the Lord had a strong band of noble workers in this town. Those who had been converted before, were now bringing in their friends, and praying with them. Thus closed our meetings here; but to be continued from house to house by the saved ones.

Zinten was my next place for work. The people had come out in great numbers, and our faith was tried. There was "no stir" in the congregation. Quite a difference was visible. A brother asked me after the meeting, "What do you think is the matter?"—"That God is saving the people," was the answer; and I knew well it was so. How strange it seems that if workers in the Lord's vineyard have had times of refreshing, they are so easily led to question when the outward manifestations suddenly change! "What is the matter?" There is a doubt in this question expressed, and it sounds as though we had not the same God of yesterday to deal with. "Not in my way, but in Thy way." Let us calmly and sweetly wait upon God — "the same yesterday, to-day, and forever" — the same God! Hallelujah! "It is not by power, nor by might, but by My Spirit, saith the Lord." Zinten was a small place, with big sins, and when the Sabbath came we opened the hall at 5 P. M. I had been very sick during the night, with a high fever, and was no better at four in the afternoon. Three of the brethren came to my bed and said: "The people expect you to preach; what shall we tell them?" "I will tell them the word of God at five o'clock; and now, dear brethren, pray, if so be the will of God, I shall arise as soon as you leave the room." The three brethren prayed to God, and then left the room. I arose and dressed, and once more I bowed before my great Heavenly Father, and committing myself — body and soul — into His hands, I asked Him, for Jesus' sake, to give me the victory over the body, and then I praised Him aloud for the victory we were going to have at the meeting.

When I met the brethren, I was quite strong to preach. My text for the afternoon was Luke xix. 10. We had not to wait very long before the glory of the

Lord appeared and filled the house. The cry for pardon rose to heaven from many hearts, and the sermon was brought to a timely close; and dismissing the congregation, I invited all those to remain who were in real earnest about the salvation of their immortal souls; but insisted that all others should retire. Thirty-five unconverted men and women remained in the hall, and after a short exhortation to them, we bowed to pray. I asked all to pray for themselves. A wonderful blessing prevailed then. The prayers were clear, and souls made sure. The victory was complete, and the bulwarks of the enemy had been stormed, and the banner of Jesus unfurled, and the shout of victory went up to heaven from the hearts of all who had sought and found the Lord.

Monday, the meeting was continued. I preached on Naaman the Syrian, and after the sermon, again an invitation was extended to seekers, and again the Lord glorified His name in the salvation of many who remained and sought the Lord. This was the last meeting at Z——.

Before leaving for Konigsberg, the saved ones had started a praise meeting, and I heard the testimonies they gave in honor of the Redeemer.

The Ancient City of the Kings. — Kant's City.

Konigsberg has a large population, and a hall was secured to seat from 2500 to 3000 persons. It had a stage and niches, very suitable for our meetings. The meetings were to last three days, and three meetings each day. The day meetings were not appreciated, but the evening meetings were good, and the hall filled. After each meeting an invitation was given for seekers to retire to the niches, and we met with a hearty and healthy response. Thanks be to God for those who from this place shall meet in heaven!

I returned to Berlin after the meetings had been closed, and I could praise the Lord for His wonderful manifestation of love and power during my time in East Prussia, and I could see how in so many different ways the same results had been obtained. The last meetings at K—— were not accompanied with the same outward signs as those in other places, but the number converted stood not behind any of the others. Oh, how much do we learn, if but our eyes be stayed on Jesus! I can afford to wait on Him, and He never failed to show me His glory in due time. Praise His name, oh my soul, for He is worthy to be praised!

On the way to Berlin, I had to visit one other small town, to preach there, and the Lord blessed me there very much, and a number of souls were converted to

God. One father brought his two sons—both married—to the inquiry room. Both seemed sincere, and confessing their sins, confessed the Saviour. I stopped over night with a brother, and I was just retiring, when I heard some one knocking against the window-pane. I opened the door to see who it was. One of those two sons, who had confessed the Saviour at the meeting, wanted to see me. He was in great sorrow, and wept. He begged me to hear him. He felt he must pour out his heart to some one, and pray once more with me, for the enemy had been sore pressing him. I prayed with him, and he was so filled, that, weeping for joy, he threw himself on my neck and kissed me. Truly God spoke peace to my soul, and gave him the victory over sin and death.

Saturday, the 26th, I returned to Berlin. My dear wife seemed to have completely recovered her health. The nine months in Europe had, thanks to God, not been without effect upon her, although for a time it seemed that the loss of our children would take away all hope for her recovery.

CHAPTER XV.

MY RETURN TO CHILI, TAKING WITH ME A GERMAN COLONY.

WE had long given up the idea of returning to the United States, but ever since our darling children had gone to God, our thoughts had wandered back to our beloved Chili,—only we did not expect to return to Valparaiso, fearing that the old trouble would come back. We hoped and prayed that the Lord would open a field in the more southern part of Chili. Our prayers soon were to be answered. Through the Chilian minister at Berlin, we received a letter from Paris, from an agent of the same government, who asked me whether I would return to Chili, and if so, try to take with me a German Colony, and in this case I should receive a free passage for myself and wife to Chili. We prayed over the matter, and it appeared clear that God might use me to bring to Chili a good colony of Christian and industrious people. Our minds were soon settled on the question, and I made my intention known to some of the people in Berlin and East Prussia. I received many letters from such as were willing to go, taking good care to select Christian people, and in the colony to represent every trade, as well as farmers.

Twenty-six families were to meet me in Hamburg, and twenty-seven more at Bordeaux, and about eighty more were to follow after the rainy season, seven months later, as they could not get ready for the ship. Those going by the way of Hamburg, were to meet me there on Thursday, the 7th of February. As I was packing our trunk, quite unsuspectingly, a police officer entered the room and arrested me in the name of the king. On inquiry, I found that I had, unknowingly, violated one of Bismarck's laws concerning emigration. It had been forbidden, and yet I had engaged those families. This was a great trial, and rather a sad parting impression upon me on leaving my "Fatherland"; but I must obey the law, and pay the penalty. I was fined $200. Some friends who had heard about it in visiting my good wife, collected at once, and raised more than was necessary. Countess W. contributed $200, and a grandchild of the old Marshall "Vornarts"-Blucher, gave $100 more. Surely, some trials and afflictions await us everywhere, and while the Lord permitted this to befall me, I feel to pray God for more wisdom, and an open eye, and make no complaint. Many times we bring trials upon ourselves, when God had nothing to with it. The Lord will bring it about and then we have the Lord's deliverance; but He will not forsake us even in the former case — only we feel like a child which puts its finger into the fire to find out what it is.

Father won't punish it, but tells us, "Don't do it again."

This delayed us in Berlin two days. When we arrived in Hamburg, we had only just time to visit once more the graves of our children. We realized so fully God's presence, that while the tears flowed, sweet peace and comfort reigned within. We had ordered two marble slabs, and when we stood at the graves they had already been placed upon them. The words inscribed were only these: "John xvi. 16: A little while." Leaving the spot, probably never to look upon it again, I pressed the hand of my precious companion and whispered: "A little while."—"Yes, a little while," she replied, "and all is well." Then we entered a coach and drove back to the city, and to the wharf where the steamer was ready to take us to England, there to meet our steamer for South America. Our colonists were all on board in due time, and happy.

The Father of a Large Family of Big Little Ones.

Thousands of questions were asked, and I felt happy to answer all I could; sometimes, however, it was impossible to do that. Then the children would come and ask me questions, and I had to stand it all; sometimes I thought they were more inquisitive than the "big children." The big ones would know all about the Arauco Indians, while the little ones were satisfied to know that we had plenty of nice "dolls" in that country.

A boarding-house had been secured for them here, and I had also cabled to England and arranged everything for their reception there, and I was held responsible by some, for all the "poor dishes," bitter coffee, and stale bread, and hard beds, and a lot of other things that I never found out; but things went on splendidly after all. I found sufficient opportunity "to do" for them.

We soon had embarked, and were under way,— no baggage missing. Half-way across the Channel, many were sea-sick. Some thought it was the steamer's fault; others, the rough weather; again, some thought "I did it"; but when we stepped on shore, all were happy again. Only two days we need wait in Liverpool. The Chilian Government provided us with a free pass to Chili, and also contracted to give to each family, one yoke of oxen, with cart and American plow; one hundred boards for building purposes; forty kilogrames nails; one cow, with calf; fifteen dollars per month for one year, and physician free for two years; and to each family, 120 acres of good land; and sixty acres more for each male member above twelve years. Conditions: That what each colonist received in cash, or cattle, and the passage money, is to be paid for in eight years, without interest. The government has fulfilled her contract to the letter.

We embarked for Chili on the 13th of February, 1884, on board the *Cotopaxi*. The passage across the ocean was a splendid one, and the emigrants behaved well. Services were held every Sabbath on deck. In Bordeaux, we received the rest of our party for Chili. One little child died before reaching Brazil, and one was born into the world. The parents called the little girl "Cotopaxi." In Rio Janeiro, myself and wife, as well as a number of colonists, visited the city. I called on some of the missionaries and spent the evening with them. The steamer left the following day, at noon. Before returning to the ship, we took lunch at the same hotel where we stopped about a year ago. The same waiter was there, and he recognized us at once. His first question was: "And where are your nice little boys?" — "They are with Jesus, my friend, — God has taken them home." My wife smiled, but her eyes filled with tears. She told me afterwards: "I suppose we can never be spared the question, and it pains; but oh, God is good! They are with Jesus."

Once more we passed through the Straits of Magellan; but they were as dismal and gloomy looking as a year ago; and passing out at the west entrance, we encountered a heavy head gale, and the steamer worked heavily — not making five miles an hour.

In five days more we landed — on the 28th of March — in Talcahuana, to discharge our human freight. All were safely landed. None were ill, and all looked happy. Some had brought money with them, and I exchanged it and got a good price for it. The government officials conducted us to the railroad station, and we took train for the interior. The first stopping place was Concepcion. The colonists staid at the soldiers' barracks. This was trying to some, but could not be helped; and, besides, they understood all before leaving their old home, and but little complaint was made. Soon we were on our way to Angol, where we received our outfits and guides.

Crossing the Coast-Cordillera. — The New Colony.

After a long rest of fifteen days, each family took charge of their carts and oxen, stowed their baggage and provisions, and now the whole train started on a three days' journey to the interior. Many of these good people had never driven oxen, and the men got out of patience with these docile animals. The children would cry, and the mothers lose patience, so in a sense they were all children. However, we safely reached our destination — our new home, — a beautiful spot, on the western slopes of the Coast-Cordillera of Nahuelbuta, and on the map called Contulmo, situated near a lake seven leagues long, but only one league in breadth. We found some natives there who had rented some land from the government. The huts, or ranchos, they lived in, had been bought for the colonists, so we found shelter at once, — the natives moving to other parts in the country.

I had gone out with them intending to stay in the colony, if so be the Lord's will, and accept land for myself, and commence school and mission work at the earliest possible date. Besides this, I desired to make arrangements for other families who desired to come over from Germany, but could not get ready for the first expedition. There were about eighty families in East Prussia who desired to come, besides many of the relatives of those with me now. We were to form, however, the only colony in those parts, and found that all those coming after us were to be settled a day's journey from Contulmo, to the south, and on the eastern side of the Coast-Cordillera, so as to place that mountain range between us and them. I at first felt a little uncomfortable about that arrangement, as I thought it would limit my field of labor too much to labor a lifetime among so few. But I thought to utilize our forces for mission work — something at the back for future development of the work among natives. The farm was to be the source of supplies for myself and family; accordingly I put my hand to the plow, and with the help of a native, with whom I contracted, put in the seeds for next year's harvest.

During the succeeding months, it became clear to me that I could not do farming work, pastoral work, and teaching day-school, all alone. The government promised to build a school-house, and I told them that I would send for a teacher. They desired me, however, to assume the responsibility of the school, to which I consented. Accordingly I sent for a teacher, who arrived from the United States in due season.

In the meantime the Lord had visited our house with a great blessing. In the month of July, a daughter was born to us.

Settling the Colonists in Their New Homes.

Services were begun from the first, and a weekly prayer-meeting established, to be held in different places each Wednesday evening. Both meetings were well attended, according to circumstances. The school-house was almost finished, and the colonists had done their field-work long ago, and harvest-time had come close to hand. Things looked cheerful, with one exception. Among the number of people we had brought with us, were some whom I designated "black sheep," and they caused us great trouble. I was not so much disappointed, as I felt sorry for them; but we would look to God and pray. However, a community is never without such. We learned that lesson in our turn.

When the teacher at last arrived, the government made an arrangement with him to pay him out of the treasury, $1.50 per child; but less than fifteen in school at a time. Only a few weeks for consideration was given, when our teacher thought this not to be the place for his work, nor a school, and that he might be able to do more good in the city. This was a great trial. He received a call to our college at Concepcion.

When we were alone once more, I saw that I could not take upon myself the work, and a trip to Santiago, our mission headquarters, became necessary, and there the brethren were consulted. Considering the circumstances, it was thought best to abandon the field at present, allowing the colonists to develop a self-supporting work among themselves, after two years more work on their farms, and then send a man to them. But I myself was to be sent back to my old field of labor — at Valparaiso. My dear wife had completely recovered her health, and since our return, had improved, so as to justify my return to Valparaiso, even in consideration of that question.

The Needs of Valparaiso.

In order now to put the work there on a firm footing, and to gather to a home my Methodist Church, and continue the work as I had done for three years, the incumbrances of those years, which kept the work from being properly organised on a broad platform, must be removed; such as renting unsuitable halls — too small, and not in the right location — and paying high rents. Valparaiso is situated along the sea-shore, and in order to make room for streets and buildings, the hills back of it — or rather, part of them — being dumped into the sea, and the houses built thereupon. This accounts for the high cost of the ground, high rents, etc., in the best parts of the city. Business houses are chiefly erected on this "made ground," and no provision is made for large halls, if we could be ever so willing to pay high rents; and such as would be rented are only large rooms, at best, badly located for Christian work. We must, then, call upon the friends of Bishop Taylor's missions in South America, to supply our "Building Fund Society," with means to put up our necessary buildings in Valparaiso, as we had done at Iquique, and Coquimbo, and Concepcion (just starting),— Valparaiso being the most important station on West Coast for a thoroughly Methodist work.

When this was clear to our minds, the brethren said: "Then, Bro. Krauser, you must go and tell the friends at home what the Lord is doing down here for us, but more especially in your work in Valparaiso, as it is for that place you require the money." After much prayer and fasting, during which latter exercise I experienced great blessings, it was made plain to me. My dear wife was consulted by letter, and she consented to the short separation — for the Master, "and the glory of God,"— as she added in her written reply. "It seems so hard," she said, "but when I remember Jesus and the work here in Chili, I say, Yes."

From Santiago I returned to our home, and made preparation for the journey.

Divine Services at the Colony.

I preached in Contulmo once more before leaving Chili, and I had the great satisfaction, after the service was closed, to have a brother and sister come up to me and say: "We will continue our Sunday services. We will, by the help of God, go and hold meetings wherever we are invited." The first appointment for the following Sabbath was made in my presence. God will be with them, for both are soundly converted to God. They are now waiting for the time to come that they shall be able to call upon us to send them the right man in due season.

Before returning to Santiago, I visited those colonists who had since arrived from Germany, and I found about one hundred families, nearly all from the East of Germany. The most of that number had either heard me preach the Gospel on my visit to East Prussia, or through others heard my name in connection with this project of colonization, so I felt at home among them, and they were glad to see me. All were willing to support a preacher as soon as they would be settled, and in some way open a market for their produce.

CHAPTER XVI.

THE FUTURE OF CHILI.—SOMETHING ABOUT THE LAND AND ITS PEOPLE.

In a few years these regions will present a very different look. Towns and villages are springing up all over the Araucanian territory, so that even now the farmer finds a market. A railroad through this same country will be completed in 1887, connecting the interior with the larger cities of the land, and with all the seaports on the West Coast. Then it will be the time for us to take up this work in the interior, not only among the foreigners, but also among the natives, and the country will produce abundant resources for our self-supporting missions among the people.

The people of Chili, religiously, are in a sad condition. Three hundred years ago the Spaniards brought with them the Roman priests,— the worst calamity that can befal any nation. The people have been priest-ridden ever since, and the result to-day is, that the poor are terribly degraded, and in the lowest sense, superstitious, and with but little sense of honor; while the middle classes and the rich are marching fast toward infidelity. They are nothing. They are not Catholics;

but from the standpoint of Romanism, as having seen it practised by its representatives for three hundred years, they judge the religion of Jesus Christ, and "the Christ" himself. These facts make the work a hard one — more difficult than the work among the heathen of other lands. And yet, Chili is one of the most liberal countries in South America, and foremost in internal development, and most settled in government; and the recent changes that have taken place — the introduction of the civil marriage law, the legalizing of religious worship of the different branches of the Protestant Church — all speak well for Chili; but if any one has watched closely the recent struggles of the "Liberal party" to separate church and state, one could not help but see that it was not simply an effort to get rid of Romanism, but to get rid of all religious obligations — to get rid of Jesus Christ — to get rid of God, as one has said, "I defy God"!

Next to nothing has been done by missionary societies to avoid this tide of infidelity which bade fair to sweep a nation out of existence into hell. A few noble men, like Dr. T. of Valparaiso, and Dr. S. of the American Bible Society, have exercised an influence for good that should not be underrated, and helped on the coming of the recent remarkable events in the history of Chili.

When seven years ago this grand and brave and God-fearing and God-trusting man, William Taylor, sent down to the coast of South America, forty-five noble workers — preachers and teachers, — he placed them into a workshop to do the hardest kind of work that ever missionaries were called upon to do; but a work that could be done — yes — can be done in the name of Jesus. I say the hardest kind of work, considering the resources at hand. Not the resources of an India. With a transient foreign population, changing every few years, and not even caring to have their children educated in this country, although now an offer was made to establish good schools,— because of the bad influence their children were exposed to — the influence of badly-managed native children — the influence of the corruption that foreigners themselves introduced into the country. Here we found no English laws or English language, and foreigners not expecting nor intending to make this country their home, and a country thoroughly Romanized. Now, we have been working hard to get the children of foreigners into our schools, for a beginning; and next, to offer to natives the chances for a liberal education, in which we have grandly succeeded; and have mostly natives now in our schools. Considering the aforesaid, William Taylor, as well as his workers, soon found it to be necessary to establish good schools everywhere, and use them as an entering wedge, to do in the future an aggressive religious work. Can any one imagine with what carefulness, wisdom, and patience, we needed to do this work? No, I think our friends cannot fully realize this feature in its every aspect; but one who has been observing the untiring, incessant, hard labor of that noble band in Copiapo, Iquique, Coquimbo, Santiago, and Concepcion, will well understand why the work has been carried on in the way and on plans, as it has been carried on. But the time has now come that the dear Lord will relieve us a bit, "striking with the same old sledge," the same "old wedge," that we placed in position seven years ago. The wedge is in to its very head, and things will split, and we must make room for it — we must enlarge our borders — enlarge the sphere of our usefulness. The wedge has done its work, and that band of workers has to face the turning-point of our work in South America, and with heavy, yet wonderfully strong and trusting and hopeful hearts, stand waiting to see the salvation of the Lord in moving the hearts of thousands of our dear friends in the United States, to give, and to liberally give, to our "building fund," to line this coast with forts for Jesus, for the preaching of the Gospel.

When Bishop Taylor was working in Coquimbo, making a full hand at the carpenters' bench, he felt for his noble workers — he felt for his beloved South America and its millions of unsaved souls; and laying down the chisel and the plane, hastened to the States. Not only Coquimbo should possess a school, but other posts of more importance must have the same. When that man of God organized the " Transit and Building Fund Society of the Taylor Self-supporting Missions," South America was uppermost in his thought. He understood the odds against us there; he knew something of the efforts put forth to maintain the field; he knew what tremendous rents we had to pay for our schools, halls, and parsonages; he knew how hard teachers were worked on half the salary that others were getting. Bro. Taylor knew something about how unfortunate we have been in getting out proper men and women for our "self-supporting work," two-thirds not understanding, evidently, the meaning of "self-supporting"; and he knew what dark hours we passed through, and what monies had to be raised among the workers, to ship the unfit back home. I am not here to judge whose fault it is, or who is to be blamed for sending persons into our field who are not fit, or returned in a few years, not able to stand the financial pressure; but I must say they are those "who sent themselves." But, thanks be to God! we have a remnant left of those who were among the first sent out by William Taylor, who have passed through deep waters; but, by the grace of God, have surmounted every obstacle; and, tried in the fiery furnace of affliction, and polished by the Spirit of burning and faith, they stand ready, on the banks of the great Pacific, to work and to die for the land that God has given them to go up and possess. Have we not the first claim on the generosity of our friends at home?

If not for our sakes, for the sake of Jesus our Saviour, and the millions of the people of South America, come and help us. We want $25,000 for our Valparaiso chapel, parsonage, and Seamen's Coffee and Reading-room, and $50,000 for our Santiago College. These are indispensable. If we expect to carry on our work successfully, these sums must be forthcoming; and laying down our request at Jesus' feet, we believe that we shall have them.

There is Bro. Baxter, working hard at Callao — an important station, — but with the same incumbrance of paying high rents, and at the same time not getting suitable houses to carry on his noble work on shore, and among seamen in that great harbor. We believe " Our Father is rich in houses and lands, and holdeth the wealth of the world in His hands," and that He has laid aside a portion of that wealth for our work in South America, and I know God is sending me to the States at this time to help gather it in, according to our present need.

Needed Workers.

What will follow next, is the demand for that class of godly men and women that such a work naturally would call for, and I am moved to say that, those being called upon to go out, should help our committee to avoid serious mistakes, as none of us are perfect in judgment, and most seriously consider the matter of coming and probably remaining for life, and to remain poor (for so it might be) from a financial point of view. Many have come, thinking to find a *ready work*, and were disappointed. Many have missed the comforts of daily life, and did not *wait* for things to change; but if the experience of those who have stood from the beginning can help us, I think something might and ought to be said.

There has been one young man who has worked but a few months, and is making only a little above his board. "How would you board?" a strange question, no doubt; but not to a Taylor missionary. Put in a straw tick, and wooden chair; dispense with "courses," and a cheap and healthful fare may be obtained. That will do for *a beginning*. But doubtless these things do not occur to all people's minds, and they might as well be spoken of and things called up by names, and price-list furnished.

BISHOP TAYLOR'S MOUNTAIN GOATS.

The Bishop wrote to me one day something about "mountain goats living on the rocks, and sniffing the air." My heartfelt reply was that I had no objections whatever to the bill of fare, except that I thought I would not grow very fat upon it. After all, it may not be a good condition to be in, for a "Taylor missionary self-supporting basis." When I first began in Valparaiso, I had no bedstead to put my bed on, but I managed to "borrow" one after a while, for down here a man must first build up a credit, before being able to "borrow." In nine months, however, things were paid for; and now, after laboring in South America since December '78, I am graciously permitted to take steerage passage to return home to raise money. Glory to God for such a privilege!

Now, if any good first-class missionary cannot reconcile himself to these facts, he or she had better not come. However, as to the continuancy of those "close-corners," I might add it is but for a season. "Have ye lacked anything?" Bishop Taylor asked me one day. — "No, brother, never!" was the joyful answer. These be sweet morsels, and not one of us would permit any one to take them from us for all the world. God doubtless has such at home, who will come and enter upon faithful work in our field, and help take this coast for Jesus; and while the Church at home is straining every nerve to raise a million for missions, let us raise *two*, one on each side. Furnish the money for our necessary buildings, and we will engage to get our living among the people where we labor.

The foreign population, — such as North Americans, Germans, and English, — for the most, do not intend to make this country their home. It is true that some have lived here from twenty to thirty years, engaged in business; but these are exceptions. Others leave this country when they have money sufficient to secure them a comfortable living in the old country. Some go on account of their children, — if not grown up before the parents are able to return to Europe or the United States, they send their children to school to those countries, much preferring to have them educated out of the country, because of the influence of the natives, which is not the best. However, the natives to-day are more sensible to the needs of a liberal education, and while they strive to get it, and thus encourage that work among them, they will soon stand on a higher platform, and the foreign element will feel a higher interest in educational and Christian work than they have shown hitherto. But few consider Chili their home, and their beneficence is much regulated by it. Large sums might be invested, to enable other societies to put up their churches and mission rooms; and but for this the means might be raised in the country itself, for all the buildings we need. The Roman Catholics cannot be asked to help us, and to wait until they are duly prepared to give large sums, would cause the work to be limited incalculably.

Bishop Taylor, in his book, "Our South American Cousins," gives a very interesting report on that line, which will prove the correct statement of the aforesaid. (Chap. xv. p. 213. It is given in the words of the first pastor who came to Chili in 1845 — Rev. Dr. Trumbull). He says as follows: "Being ordained for the ministry in Valparaiso in 1845, I sailed for that place in August, and arrived on Christmas Day, Dec. 25. The prospect was anything but encouraging. It was impossible for six months to secure a room for a chapel, until at last we obtained a dark and diminutive *bedego* (storehouse). This has been our trouble during my time in Valparaiso"; but he goes on to state another fact, which corresponds exactly to my experience in 1880–83. He says: "At the end of six months, however, the dining-room of the Chili hotel was offered, which was commodious for an audience of a hundred. At the end of a year orders came from the owners in Santiago to vacate the place, on religious grounds." Now, thus the priests used their influence in just that direction; and in my time — 1880–83 — we were ejected in the same way, or exorbitant rents asked. Now Dr. Trumbull built a church, but not until he had labored nine years among the English. In my work the people are ready now to move into a home, if I had one to offer them. However, this first church was so small, that in 1869 another was built, and the old place sold to the Germans. The cost of the new church was $57,000, Chili money, and out of that sum $26,000 was paid for the lot alone, and $37,000 expended for the building. It is found, then, that land is extremely high, and the following will show something of the reason. Bishop Taylor, in his book, says (Chap. xv.): "It is a city built on more than 'seven hills,' and precipitous bluffs facing the ocean. The city has but two or three level streets (near the ship-landing and the business part of the city). This level land, on which stand all the public buildings, and most of the business houses, was mainly recovered from the sea." At this present time, there is an extensive work of that kind going on, and several acres of ground will be gained; but the prices for land will be very high, and on it we must build, in order to make the movement in some degree attractive. Now, money should not be the object to keep us from carrying on that work in Valparaiso. We must, by all means, save some; and if we can add to the numbers of the church by raising a home for the mission, we are bound to go ahead, and in the name of God, get the money. There was a time when men said it was unsafe for any one to go to the "Maintop," for they were sure to be caught by the parson, and rumsellers did poor business. Now, I thank God for that spirit among the people. I feel we must improve it until that part of the Lord's vineyard is cleansed of those terrible dens of vice. We desire to make it proverbial, as in the time when a thief stole the horse of a Methodist preacher, and he, mounting with a few farmers, overtook the thief, who, when he was bound, and heard that the horse belonged to a Methodist preacher, said: "If he had known this fact he'd never have touched the horse, for he knew that they would be after him to the end of the world, and into hell to get hold of him." Amen! praise the Lord! May God intensify the desire of Christians at home, to help put missionaries in the way of doing more work for God in reaching souls, by giving to such an object as this on my hands now.

I never felt so in my life, as I feel at present, since I am away for a season from Chili. I desire to hasten back, for I love that work — it has become a part of myself. Yes, I must look after my family. It is true that I have often been in danger; but oh, how at home I feel in this work! It is the work God called me to, and I do love it. I never loved it so much until one evening, while calling at different gambling and dancing houses, I saw a suspicious-looking individual following me close behind. He was a tall, powerful native, and I noticed he was closely watching me. I did not like the way he acted; but never dreamed of what he really intended to do. When I walked down a narrow, dark passage, to reach the mission-room, to open my meeting, I was suddenly confronted, and the man drew a long knife, about one foot long, and made the attempt to plunge it into my heart. I wore an overcoat at the time, because in it I had five large pockets, purposely made to carry quantities of tracts, in as many different languages; and when the man struck, he seemed to know where the heart was; but the knife met a large package of tracts that were in my pocket, and the shock I received caused me to stagger back a little distance. Just then I heard the shriek of a woman, and in the next moment the galloping of a horse close by; and in that moment, when the ruffian ran toward me for another trial, he was suddenly struck down by a policeman on horseback. Now, this was done quicker than I am able to write it down, and during that time, when first the man stood in front of me, until now, not a word had escaped my lips. A woman just turning a corner, stepped into the passage where I was struck, gave the signal to a policeman, who was halting on his horse, close by in the next street; and he, quick as lightning, put the spur to his horse, and appeared "just in time." The knife fell from the grasp of the assassin, and the woman picked it up and handed it to me, and I could see it was a terrible weapon. Before the man recovered, he was bound with thongs and tied to the saddle of the horse. Then the policeman requested me to follow him at once to the police station; but being well known to him, I just gave him my card, and told him that I had a meeting at the room, and that the men were waiting for me. He ordered me to appear the following morning at court.

The unfortunate prisoner was dragged off, and I hurried off to my little mission-room. It was filled with anxious souls — none knew what had passed outside; but when I told them that God had spared me to come, and once more bring the message of salvation, as one risen from the dead, the power of God came down upon those assembled, in such a wondrous way as was never witnessed in our room before. It was the most solemn hour of my life, and the Lord saved five precious souls that night. From that night I have a different experience in my feelings toward that work. Oh, if I could be able to frame it in language! but I cannot. I will say this: my soul is united to that work in Valparaiso, and I must hasten back. I love it; yes, Lord, Thou knowest I love Thee and it; for thou hast surely called me to do that work. Glory be to His precious name — the name of Jesus!

The next day the poor prisoner was sent to the penitentiary. He made no excuse, except that he said I had attempted to stab him first.

CHAPTER XVII.

MY PERSONAL EXPERIENCE.—WONDERFUL SALVATION.

My soul has been drinking all the while from the inexhaustible fountain of God's mighty love, and I am already amply repaid for the work I have undertaken; but others must drink and know my God, and what His glory is. And if by means of this book the Lord has opened to me a way for the support of my family while away from Chili, and to pay my own travelling expenses while in this country, it is only the one side of what it is to accomplish, and my Jesus and my Saviour will take care of the whole.

"O give thanks unto the Lord, for He is good, for his mercy endureth forever. Let the redeemed of the Lord say so, whom he hath redeemed from the hand of the enemy; and gathered them out of the lands, from the east and from the west, from the north and from the south. They wandered in the wilderness in a solitary way; they found no city to dwell in; hungry and thirsty, their soul fainted in them; then they cried unto the Lord in their trouble, and he delivered them out of their distresses. And he led them forth by the right way, that they might go to a city of habitations. O that men would praise the Lord for his goodness, and for his wonderful works to the children of men. For he satisfieth the longing soul, and filleth the hungry soul with goodness.

"O God, my heart is fixed: I will sing and give praise, even with my glory. Awake, psaltery and harp, I myself will awake early. I will praise thee, O Lord, among the people, and I will sing praises unto thee among the nations, for thy mercy is great above the heavens, and thy truth reacheth unto the clouds. Yea, I will tell what the Lord has done for my soul."

Early Religious Training.

In February, 1875, I heard for the first time the Gospel preached to sinners, in this country. My early religious training, if training it could be called, I received under the hands of a minister of the Lutheran Church, in Germany. He was an eloquent man, but Christless; and I do not remember a single sentence of any of his sermons preached in my hearing. They were, however, few, as I attended the public services perhaps only three times in the eighteen years of my life in Germany. Thus my religious "training" consisted of one hour a week, during a period of six weeks prior to my "confirmation." When the pastor laid his hands upon my head to bless me, and I partook of the sacred cup, I was already a hardened and careless sinner; but the music of the organ, together with the solemnity of the occasion, caused tears to start to my eyes for a moment; then all was gone, never to return again for many years. I do not even remember the verse of Scripture that was given me before leaving the altar, and the certificate was soon lost. When I returned to an uncle's house, I received some cigars, with the words: "Now you are a man, and are allowed to smoke openly before men, without fear of being punished." I felt proud, and that was all; the day of confirmation had passed, and I entered upon a career of unrestrained pleasure and sinfulness, and outspoken infidelity.

The Influence of My Mother's Life.

My poor mother was much grieved because of my conduct, and often wept, although it was long before I knew it. My mother I loved dearly, but her wonderful patience, her noble character, together with her high social refinement, were unbearable to me. In her presence alone I could be good, I thought; yet I did not wish to be in her presence. With irresistible force it drove me away, to my pleasures, to my companions. There came a time when I looked upon my mother in wonder. I could not understand how a human being could be so good, so pure, so gentle, as she was; and I envied her, and a longing after such a life would spring up in my soul; so that often, upon my bed, I caught myself bitterly weeping,— only for a moment, however, — as soon as I became conscious of the state of my feelings, I tore myself away with an effort. Then I would for some time shun the eyes of my mother. I feared she would see what was going on within me. The time came when I found out that she prayed at times. I feared her now,— that is, I strove hard to hide my bad conduct from her; yet I knew that she was only too well acquainted with me, and I would at times feel, oh, if only mother would come to me and tell me something about myself! if she would only tell me to my face that I could not deceive her! I suffered now for years, untold torments, for I felt I loved her, and I would not have grieved her for anything in the world; and yet, I could not resist sin. I stood alone, without God, without Christ, without hope in the world. I had never heard her utter a harsh word; I had never seen her impatient; but when, one day, I had grieved her very much, she came toward me with such a careworn look upon her, looking at me with such piercing eyes, yet so imploringly, it seemed I could not bear it, and bitter remorse gripped my soul. Before I could turn away, she was at my side, and had caught my hand and held it in both hers. I did not dare look her in the face, for I thought her to be an angel in the form of my own dear mother. She softly called my name, "Oscar!" and I looked up into her eyes. Oh, that moment! It stands before my soul to-day. When I looked into those blue eyes, so full of grief, and filled with tears to overflowing, and the hot drops falling down upon my hand as she held it in her dear hands, I wished myself dead. Yes, I wished then I had died. I was so sick at heart — so tired of life. Why was it that God did not send me a ray of light then? But not a word dropped from her lips. My hand dropped, lifeless, almost, to my side, and my mother had turned and left the room. I stood alone.

My Infidelity Shaken.— Trying to Get Away from God.

In that hour I knew there was a God, and this was burned down deep into my soul. The life of my mother stood in living flames of fire before me. I was crushed to the earth by the mighty evidence it furnished, and now I strove, oh, so hard, day and night, to free myself from this weight of conviction which threatened to madden my brain. I drowned my feverish heart in the cooling ocean of pleasures, but only to increase the raging of the flames within.

Dissatisfied with everybody and myself, I rushed headlong down the road to destruction. My home became too small for me — I had no rest. Day and night my mother seemed to stand before me, and I must look upon her wherever I stood, wherever I went,— and then the force of the fact, "There is a God!" I could not abate it. Miserable and sick at heart, and my infidel reasoning not able to cure the wound that I had received, and angry with the world because of its miserable weakness, I made a resolve, as a last remedy, to flee away from God — to abandon myself entirely; but not at home — not so, that my poor mother should ever know what had become of her unhappy boy, whom she loved dearest on earth. I would go to North America. I stopped only a moment to think, "What will she say?" and then I struck the cruel blow.

I left the city, and then I wrote a letter, for I did not dare to look at her face. To my great astonishment, the answer was in the affirmative. I did not know what to make of it. Was it pride? I did not know. Was it that her love to me was no longer the same? Oh, I was so miserable once more; for while I thought a mother still loved me, I might bear to live, if even in sin and shame. I hurried home. Preparations had already been made. Everything that such a mother could do had already been done for me, and my trunk stood ready. But the love of my mother had increased. When I saw her she had faded away, and how loving and kind she was! I felt the hardness of my heart, and for a time I was afraid of myself. But soon an effort set me on my feet again, and I thought I was strong: then a faint glimmer of a desire would spring up to be a better man; but only to relapse into thoughts of self.

A Broken-Hearted Mother.

The day of departure arrived. Father and mother accompanied me to the station, Berlin to Hamburg. I bade them good-by, as I felt it to be forever, or rather, thought nothing concerning my ever coming back. As the train moved, my mother reached out her hands once more and said: "My Oscar, be a better boy!" Then she looked upward, but fainted, and sank in the arms of my father. These were her last words on earth to me, and thus I saw her for the last time this side of heaven. I heard the words, and I saw her faint; but I had no tears, and I strove in vain to seek relief.

On the 5th of August, 1872, I arrived in Liverpool, and on the 10th I embarked on the steamship *St. Louis* for New Orleans, La., where we arrived safely on the 1st of September. I found, of course, things much different from what I expected, and work I would not, for a long time. But at last, when all my resources had been exhausted, and no hope of obtaining money without work could be entertained, I walked forty miles, down the Mississippi River, and began work on a sugar plantation. A German of my type had induced me to go with him, promising me employment through a friend, in the sugar-house. I had been deceived, however, and I was compelled to work in the field. In three days after, I was thrown out of the lodging-house, sick with the fever, and unable to work. Somehow, I managed to reach New Orleans, and I was picked up on the street and sent to the hospital. A most miserable life followed now. For more than a year I was in the hospital, off and on. I had become totally unfit for any kind of work; every three or four weeks I was taken to the hospital again, where I stayed, perhaps a week or more. Only half restored, I left the hospital, for I had no rest, and upon my bed the most horrible thoughts tormented me. I felt I was forsaken and alone. I thought above all other things, about my mother, so far away from me. Memory was consuming me with a slow fire, and yet I was not relieved,—I still lived.

In America.— Sick and in Rags.

In those hours I thought death would be a relief,— I mean those hours when I wished to work and could not, and when I walked like a shadow through the streets of the city, and my eyes fell by and by on ragged clothing and torn boots,— I mean those hours when I looked into the yards of private dwellings, to see whether wood was piled up there, that I might work for a bit of food. It is true I had not much appetite, but just enough to desire to quench the craving of hunger. Just a little was necessary; but I was too proud to ask for it. Then those moments when I did begin to cut wood, and the axe would sink from my grasp, and I fell down on the heap, bitterly weeping, and unable to rise. Then a charitable hand would touch me, and lead me to the street, and send me again to the hospital. And in those hours, when I wished for death,— what if God had then cut me off? Oh, how my soul blesses the God of heaven that in His mercy He permitted me to live at all, and when He permitted me to sink so deep in degradation and sin, to finally raise me up, to give me life and peace and joy, and entrust to me the oracles of God, to preach the everlasting Gospel. It is to the glory of Jesus, my Saviour, for ever and ever!

And how could I regain health and strength again? I had given up all hope of ever recovering,— those terrible fevers would not loose their hold on me; and how did I spend my nights? Oh, wretched life of sin, away from God, no one pitied me! I thought I needed sympathy — human sympathy — and I cursed mankind. My nights were spent in the empty cars on the railroad track, shaking with ague, and nothing but rags to cover my frame. The hand of God was heavy upon me, but He knew me best. God knew best what was in me — He knew to apply the medicine. It was bitter, and I was farther away from God than ever, and yet wanted it so. I wanted to get away from Him, but I did not want to suffer like that. I did not want to believe in Him, but I cursed Him to His face! I did not want to know anything of God, but I blamed Him for the misery in which I was now, and cast up to Him my education, my breeding; and now to be so shamefully reduced! Oh, I found it hard to fight against God! I would rage, and by force shake off my weakness and disease; but my sins and my deserted home rose now like mountains up before me, and I sank back in despair. But at last I made an effort to escape this terrible climate. Sick at heart, and feeble in body, I left this State, walking on foot, but now and then, during the night, trying to get on some train, and sitting outside as best I could, between the cars, until I was detected by some one, and compelled to walk again. Thus I reached the State of O.: and now deliverance should come. May I be spared the bitter remembrance of the past; but notwithstanding, God must be glorified, and His sweet presence stills the tears, and causes me in the midst of them, to rejoice with joy and singing. If so be that the fountains of the deep break up once more, the floods of heavenly glory are overwhelmingly precious, and I join the chorus of fire, Redeemed, redeemed, yes, redeemed through the blood, the precious blood of the Lamb Christ Jesus, from all the filthiness and sins of my life, and cleansed from all indwelling corruption through sanctification by faith.

Light from Calvary's Cross.

Suffice it, then, to say: the Gospel of Jesus was brought to me. Curiosity led me to hear "common people" preach, and to see a woman pray. Dear Father Webb, dear Sister Joice, how can I help mentioning their names, that are so dear to me on earth! with my tears I would burn them into these pages; for has not God found them worthy in the Lamb's book of life, and shall I not look upon them once more in the presence of my God, on His white throne? Shall I not be there when they shall bear me in their arms and lay me down, a trophy, down at Jesus' feet, as a brand plucked from the fire?

The former was an employee of one of the railroad companies at C——, and the dear sister a companion in the labors of love.

After six long weeks, I felt constrained to bow down for the first time before God. I could not keep away from the meetings. I must go to hear, although others laughed at me and mocked me. But while I look up to God with thankful heart for this help, I bless His name for the hour when first I knelt down in prayer, after the brother had spoken on Christ's death on the cross. I could bear it all; but when he told how that Christ had said: "Father, forgive these murderers, for they know not what they do," I could bear it no longer,—I turned, smitten to the heart, to see whether I could rise and go away, to be alone. But just then Sister J. knelt down right beside me, and all present were asked to join in prayer. She prayed, and it seemed she prayed for me alone. I felt it, yes, I was not mistaken—she named me to God. Oh, how I felt the eye of God piercing me that moment, when this sister prayed: "O God! save this young man! save him now, and put Thine everlasting arm beneath him!"

My heart was broken to pieces under the stroke of the hammer of God's wondrous love. Still there was darkness, but I seemed to stretch out my hand and grope, yet quickly I would withdraw my hand and say: "You are not meant, don't think it for a moment." Then my sins came rushing forward. I could bear it no longer. I started to my feet and made for my room. But the brother had watched me well. He met me just in time in front of the door, and taking one of my hands, he asked, imploringly: "Young man, will you be a Christian?"

When I was able to look up, I seemed that moment to understand the question. Like a flash it crossed my darkened soul; but I had caught it. It was that I had tried to grasp during prayer a moment ago. Yes, glory to God! I knew, now, Christ had died for me, and stood to break down the middle wall of partition in my behalf. I saw in flaming letters before me, the words of my own Saviour, "It is finished!" I firmly grasped the brother's hand, and said: "By the help of God, I will!" Oh, how I wished that moment that the good brother would wait and talk with me; but the Lord knew better what was wanted, — he was prevented, and left me to myself; only saying these words, which I will not forget any more: "Remember, every night at twelve o'clock I am on my knees praying for you. Until next Sunday I am night-watch all the week, in the station.

A Personal Fight with Satan. — The Terribleness of Sin.

I entered my room and thought to pray for the first time — earnestly to pray that God for Christ's sake might forgive me my sins. When I knelt down, it seemed I could not speak the name of God, and great darkness fell upon me. The load of sin was too great for me, and I was in agony, and struggled for utterance, but the more I struggled to pray, the more terrible appeared my sins. I began again to bemoan myself, and wept because I was so miserable and unhappy. Still my sins rose up before me again, and brought before me the fact that these were the cause of all, and that I must have peace with God. Thus I wrestled and prayed, and agonized, yet no light came. I could not bring myself to the point to exercise faith, and perhaps I was not quite letting myself go, or had not yet, from my heart, renounced the world. I was not yet humble, and God, in His mercy, smote me still. I cried out: "Slay me, but save me!"

I lay thus in my room until Friday afternoon, at four P. M. I had taken but little food all this time, and I felt my strength giving way. But I was determined not to let go. I said to myself, continually: "Better die than live a moment in sin." I was feeble in body; I could not bear any more strain, — weary and tired, I sat on my bed, when once more I knelt in prayer, and then, as never before, I cried out to God in the words of the Scripture which I had so often heard: "God be merciful to me, a sinner!" and like a flood of light it dawned upon me, and I added: "Yes, Lord, right now I believe! I believe!"

The work was done. The load of sin was lifted off. I was free, and I knew it. I jumped up from where I was kneeling, and praised God with a loud voice,—so loud that all in the house could hear me, and I was so happy that I laughed and wept at the same time. Some of the people in the house looked at me in astonishment. Then I heard one young man say: "Oh, he is crazy! He'll be all right soon, and we'll have him back among the old friends." I replied at once, and said: "No, never! You may have all the friends, all the world, and all that is in the world, but I have Christ; and, thanks be to God, I have Him now!" I was converted: I belonged to God, and more, I had said on my knees, "Lord, I will preach Thy Gospel to every creature!" and the Lord held me to my word.

Every day for about three weeks, I had been permited to read the Bible and exhort the prisoners at the county jail in the city. God blessed me in these labors, and gave me many precious souls. Thus the Lord prepared me to work among the lost and the lowest, right from the beginning of my Christian course. The Bible, which had never come to my hand before, was my companion day and night now, and I devoured its contents. My soul was full of joy and praises to God.

One day, however, a former companion provoked me to anger, and oh, how miserable I was when I felt it spring up within me! I prayed to God at once, to help me, and I was helped instantly, so that the young man did not perceive what was going on within me. But when he continued troubling me, the same uprising came back and I felt sorry. I prayed, but I found it would overcome me. I did not know what to do, yet I prayed. But there came a moment, suddenly, and quicker than I can tell, when I raised my hand and struck the man in his face. Long I had withstood the rising of my temper, and now I was unhappy again, under condemnation. I hurried to my room and there prayed, and repented of what I had done. I felt terribly, for I thought nothing should ever come up between me and my God any more. I would serve Him who had done so much for me, to the end of my life, cost what it may. I was happy and satisfied once more, although I felt ashamed and grieved that I had so soon offended the loving Saviour, and I prayed earnestly that I might be kept watching, and looking to Jesus. I read about Peter on the water, walking, and I thought this stood for a warning to me not to do like him; but that by faith I could be kept up, looking to Jesus.

The Discovery of a Hidden Enemy.

However, I had now constant trouble with my temper, and trouble with so many other things. Those came of pride in the same way, and evil thinking, and I would pray and wrestle with God, and in tears I would cry out: "O Lord, Thou knowest I do not want those things in me! Thou knowest I hate the very appearance of evil! I want to be all Thine! I want to be holy and pure!" From this time I experienced such intense hungering and thirsting for more of God, and to be a better Christian, as I termed it in my prayers, that I was almost constantly praying; and yet this terrible fight going on within me all the time. No one knew what was going on within me. My outward life did but show the strictest consistency with the teachings of the Scriptures. I carried my New Testament about with me to every place, and if I had but one minute's time, I would look into it, and read, and compare my own heart with it, and as I drank in every word, the hunger for a far different life — a higher and purer life, — only increased. Not that I was conscious of anything wrong that I had done all this time, since I struck the young man, either in word or deed; but these inward troubles, these evil uprisings, these movings in my own heart, oh, they tormented me so much! Day and night I was praying, and sometimes my heart was so full of joy that I wept, and clapped my hands, and praised God for hours in my room; and then those constant victories that I had over myself, strengthened me wonderfully; for never had the evil yet gotten the upper hand; but I had so much grace given me that I could keep it all down. Still there was this gnawing in my heart for something, I did not know what, and I could not find it out, except that I felt bad when those evils rose within me, and I was blessed again in a few minutes after. Sometimes, though, I would be so grieved that I wept for hours, and prayed, because I seemed to be wrapt up entirely in self.

Now, along with all this, I would sometimes lie awake upon my bed a long time and weep for joy, and clap my hands, and meditate upon my blessed Saviour and His wonderful word. It seemed as though I could then penetrate the meaning of Scripture better than ever, and the grandest and sweetest Christian life would loom up before me, and I would stretch out my hand to God as though trying to pull down to me, with all my might, this something that I wanted to make me well-pleasing in His sight. The morning came, and it was the same again. This lasted for four long, long, weary months. I was happy,— but oh, I wanted something; and I knew now that the state of my inner man kept me from possessing God entirely, as I thought. But then, I was comforted again by hearing the testimonies of others. They seemed to be happy, too, and lived a Christian life, and they even sometimes spoke of these things that so troubled me; but this was something I could not do. I could not speak of it, for when I heard them speak of these things, I felt more ashamed and was more sure that this was wrong in me, and I thought I could never really glorify my Father. Then grief intensified, and new struggles ensued.

THE REPRESSION THEORY. — THE DISAPPOINTMENT.

But at last I got hold of something that brought rest to me, in a certain way; that is, I "would not" trouble so much as I used to, and bear as others bore; and that was this: I seemed to gather from the experiences of others, that this way was "the Christian's warfare." I took hold of this as a drowning man would a straw. If others, older in experience, and so many in number, have the same experience, then of course it is this way with everybody. The idea gave me some comfort, and now my mind was quite made up to fight the good fight of faith — to work out my salvation with fear and trembling — and fight, and fight, the evil in me, till the last breath of life. By the help of God, I should! Yes — I was determined to be and remain a Christian, and more so now than ever. So this was, then, the Christian warfare, and I settled down on that, and said to myself, "Now, you might have saved yourself a good deal of trouble." This was all settled on an evening when quite alone with God, and my heart was overflowing with gratitude toward my Heavenly Father for revealing to me His wondrous love, mercy, and longsuffering. I know the Lord had much patience with me, and the feeling of humility at this time was sweet.

That night I shall never forget, because in it all my new hopes had vanished away, and all my old fears had revived. The same troubles, the same uprisings; and no matter how strongly I would plead the idea of the "Christian warfare," my inner man did not pay any attention to it, and I found that Christ did not reconcile Himself to the sin within me. Everything would now come up; but especially with the lust of the flesh was I troubled, and the enemy would trouble me in a way and with thoughts of things that I never had when actually living in sin. I threw myself across my bed. I wet the pillows with my tears, and told the Saviour the old story: "Thou knowest I hate these things from the bottom of my inmost soul. I do not want anything filthy in my heart. I want Thee, and only Thee, to reign in my soul." There was no confession to outward sin, for God kept me from yielding to any temptation; but I knew that those things did not arise from the outside. I knew only too well they came from within, and I cried again to God to give me a pure and holy heart. I was well nigh worn out in body. My strong crying upon my bed, and my burning desire for more of God to the cleansing of my heart, was so intense that I thought I would be ill, and I asked God in earnest prayer, and in faith, for light and help.

Now, I had not only testified for Jesus in jails, but also spoke in the name of Christ in the penitentiary of this State, to the prisoners there; and one day, after leaving the chapel, I noticed a prisoner walking up to an officer on guard, close by where I stood talking with him. The officer gave me a sign to stop, and the prisoner turned toward me and handed me a little pamphlet. His eyes were full upon me, and filled with tears. It seemed like a dream to me. Before I could tell what I had received, the prisoner had left me, for he was just permitted to give me this paper after the officer had examined it, but was not allowed to speak to me. Somehow, I felt it was something for me, and I could hardly await the time to see what it contained.

A Prisoner Gives Me the "Guide to Holiness."

Once more I stood just over my bed, for I had taken no time to sit down to read; and then with trembling hand, I unfolded the pamphlet and read the *Guide to Holiness*. I was struck with the "Holiness." I had not seen this particular word in such large letters before, and I hastily turned over the first leaf, and there once more I read " Holiness unto the Lord." So many thoughts now crowded my mind. This book in the penitentiary! Somehow it had found its way there, and then, those tearful eyes, that man in the prison-yard, so full of emotion and love, it seemed. With an effort I drove away these pictures, and I read part of the "Experience of Hester Ann Rogers," and another part of Fletcher. I had never heard those names before, and I did not care who they were; but what I read there thrilled my soul, and with trembling hands did I hold that blessed little paper, and with quivering lips, and with a heart full to overflowing, I perused those lines again. "My own experience!" "My own desire!" "My own experience!" I could only cry out again and again. "O my God!" I cried, and completely overcome with this wonderful power that flooded my soul, I fell on the floor,— the book had dropped from my grasp. I felt the color of my face change, and a tremor ran through my entire frame; and then, stretching out my arms to heaven, my eyes fixed on Jesus, in Person, as it seemed, and "O my great Redeemer! my blessed Jesus!" was all I could say for a time.

Then burst forth that long pent-up desire of my soul, — the light had come, and now I lay drinking, drinking from the fountain of life. I opened my soul to God, and said, now, simply: "All, all is mine, blessed Jesus! I now believe! I now believe Thou dost cleanse me from my sin!"

The lines that spoke concerning Fletcher, had the text from John, "And the blood of Jesus Christ His Son cleanseth 'me just now' from all sin." It was written in that way, and the words "me just now" fastened themselves upon me, and thus I stood before God. "The blood just now cleanseth me from all my sins."

A Real Inwrought Holiness.

It seems now as though I cannot go on to say more. How can I say more?

I arose quietly, as though I dare not disturb the solemnity of the moments. I felt as though the room was filled with the angelic host, looking on in wonder and amazement to behold the mighty work of a crucified Redeemer, whose name is "Wonderful, Everlasting Father, Prince of Peace." Scarcely touching the floor with my feet, I walked slowly to and fro in the room, silently pressing my hands upon each other again and again. All was so quiet about me, and heavenly peace seemed to reign. There was not that same outward manifestation of joy as at the time of my conversion, but a peace, calm as a river, flowing deep down in my inmost soul — a peace that passed all understanding. I cannot explain it, but I knew it was there. I possessed a real, inwrought holiness. Without a sound scarcely, proceeding from my lips, I merely whispered: "Glory to God! glory, glory, glory!" Then I sat down upon my bed, intoxicated with Divine love. Then my physical man called for his rights, and when my head touched the pillow, I fell asleep, and oh, what a sleep! like a man who had not been able to sleep for weeks, and dreaded the coming of the night, but had suddenly been healed and rested in sleep from a long and weary sickness. Sweet, refreshing sleep.

Thus the peace of God settled down into my soul, and when I awoke late in the evening, it was there — the same blessed, real holiness,— the love of God made perfect in my soul; and as I write down these lines, I find it is there still, but deeper, and sweeter, and more precious than ever before. Wondrous love! Wondrous keeping power of the mighty Christ! Glory be to His dear name! To Him belongeth all the glory; and if, in reading these lines, a soul is helped, a soul is rescued, a soul is filled with all the fullness of God and the power of a holy life, then the glory of God shall shine but brighter, and next we meet around the throne in glory, to crown HIM Lord of all.

THE CHRISTIAN WITNESS

AND

ADVOCATE OF BIBLE HOLINESS.

EDITED BY

Revs. W. McDonald, Joshua Gill, and G. D. Watson, D.D.

PUBLISHED TWICE A MONTH.

$1 a Year, postage included.   To Clergymen, 75 cts.

In addition to the editorial management of the above, besides articles from some of the best writers on Holiness, the WITNESS contains letter from Missionaries in nearly every part of the world.

BISHOP WM. TAYLOR

is one of our regular contributors, and others of his African party will keep our readers posted on the great African Mission. Bishop Taylor's Transit Fund is regularly reported in our columns. In fact, we intend that

The WITNESS shall take the lead

in the dissemination of information regarding the progress in all parts of the world of the great Self-Supporting Mission movement, while at the same time, the main idea,

"TO SPREAD SCRIPTURAL HOLINESS OVER THESE LANDS,"

shall be prosecuted vigorously.

SAMPLE COPY FREE!

❖ NEW ❖ BOOKS ❖

SONGS OF JOY AND GLADNESS.
A new Singing Book, by W. McDonald, Joshua Gill, J. R. Sweney, and W. J. Kirkpatrick. 271 hymns: about 75 new, and the remainder the cream of other books. 40 cts. single; $4 per doz.; $30 per hundred.

LIFE OF REV. JOHN S. INSKIP,
President of the National Camp-meeting Association. By W. McDonald and J. E. Searles. Illustrated with portrait of Mr. Inskip, and lithograph of the chapel in which he was converted. Price $1.25.

CATECHISM ON CHRISTIAN PERFECTION.
By Rev. E. T. Curnick, A.M. Price 50c.

CHRISTIAN PERFECTION AS TAUGHT BY WESLEY.
By Rev. J. A. Wood, author of "Perfect Love," "Purity and Maturity," etc. Containing all that Mr. Wesley ever said on the subject, arranged and classified. Introduction by Bishop Mallalieu. Price $1.

FREDERICK WILLIAM FABER.
Selections from his prose and poetic writings. By Rev. James Mudge, late editor of the *Indian Witness*. Price 50c.

LIFE OF WILLIAM TAYLOR, BISHOP OF AFRICA.
By J. W. Hamilton, D.D. (To be issued as soon as prepared.)

TRUE PERFECTION ATTAINABLE.
A poetical exposition of the Book of Job. Price 50c.

THE FUNERAL SERVICE.
A book for Clergymen; containing appropriate Scriptures for all burial services; blank pages for records, places for outlines of sermons, choice selections from the poets, etc. Price in cloth, 75c.; in leather, $1.

McDONALD & GILL, Publishers,
36 Bromfield St., Boston.

Holiness ✤ Writings

—of—

Rev. G. D. Watson, D.D.

HOLINESS MANUAL. 25 cts.

WHITE ROBES. 50 cts.

OUT OF EGYPT INTO CANAAN. Personal Experience. 5 cts.

WHITE ROBES (tract). 2 cts.

FRUITS OF CANAAN. 10 cts.

INDWELLING COMFORTER. 3 cts.

SCRIPTURE EMBLEMS OF THE HOLY SPIRIT. 5 cts.

THREE FS. 1 ct.

TWO CROSSINGS. 2 cts.

THAT REVIEW ARTICLE. 5 cts.

McDONALD & GILL, Publishers,

36 Bromfield St. - - - - Boston.

Holiness Books.

New Testament Standard of Piety.
By Rev. W. McDonald. With a steel portrait of the author. Price 50 cts.

Scriptural Way of Holiness.
By Rev. W. McDonald. Price 75 cts.

Marquis De Renty.
By Rev. W. McDonald. Price 60 cts.

God's Method with Man.
By Rev. B. W. Gorham. Price $1.00

Offices of the Holy Spirit.
By Dougan Clark, M.D. Price 75 cts.

The Historical Position of Wesleyan Methodism on the Subject of Holiness.
(Just issued.) By Rev. Chas. Munger. Price 10 cts.

The Second Blessing Demonstrated.
(Just issued.) By Rev. B. F. Gassaway. Price 10 cts.

Inheritance Restored.
By Rev. M. L. Haney. Price $1.00.

Love Enthroned.
By Daniel Steele, D.D. Price $1.25.

Milestone Papers.
By Daniel Steele, D.D. Price 85 cts.

Holiness Bible Readings.
By Rev. Isaiah Reid. Price 60 cts.

McDONALD & GILL,
36 BROMFIELD ST. - - - - BOSTON.

www.ingramcontent.com/pod-product-compliance
Lightning Source LLC
Chambersburg PA
CBHW021151230426
43667CB00006B/350